Jam Yesterday

Nancy Horne

Jam Yesterday:
A Leith Childhood

The Pentland Press
EDINBURGH

© Nancy Horne 1990

First published in 1990 by
The Pentland Press Ltd.,
Kippielaw, Haddington,
East Lothian, Scotland

Jacket design by Ann Ross Paterson

ISBN 0 946270 88 0

Typeset by Polyprint
Printed and bound by
Billings and Sons Ltd.,
Book Plan: Worcester

"You couldn't have it if you DID want it," the Queen said.
"The rule is, jam to-morrow and jam yesterday — but never jam
to-day."

<u>Through the Looking-Glass</u> by Lewis Carroll.

For

Charlie, Netta, Mamie, Madeline, Betty,
Jim and Jean

By the author of
<u>Love from Egypt</u>

Acknowledgements

The Steel Bonnets — The Story of Anglo-Scottish Border Reivers by George MacDonald Fraser.

Ordinary Lives 100 years ago by Carol Adams.

The Life and Times of Leith by James Scott Marshall.

Scenes of Edwardian Life by Sir Charles Petrie.

Victoria R.I. by Elizabeth Longford.

The way we were — 1900-1914 by James McMillan.

Leith Lives — Memories at Work — a look at employment between the wars.

The First day on the Somme by Martin Middlebrook.

History of the Black Watch in the Great War; The New Army; 8th Battalion Black Watch, edited by Major General A.G. Wauchope and kindly lent to me by Mr Ian McNaughton.

Dear Old Blighty by E.S. Turner.

Old Soldiers Never Die by Frank Richards, D.C.M., M.M.

The Zeppelin Fighters by Archibald Whitehouse.

Fire Over England by H.G. Castle.

The Great War and Modern Memory by Paul Fussell.

Life in Britain between the wars by L.C.B. Seaman.

The Last Picture Shows, Edinburgh, by Brendan Thomas.

Those were the days — A Photographic Album of daily life in Britain published by J.M. Dent & Sons Ltd.

The World we left behind by Robert Kee.

Later than we thought by René Cutforth.

With grateful thanks to Dr William Lumsden, M.B., Ch.B., M.R.C.G.P., M.P.S. and Dr Andrew C. Douglas, M.B., Ch.B, F.R.C.P.(Edin.), both of whom gave invaluable assistance with medical information.

Photographs

HARRISES and RUTHERFORDS

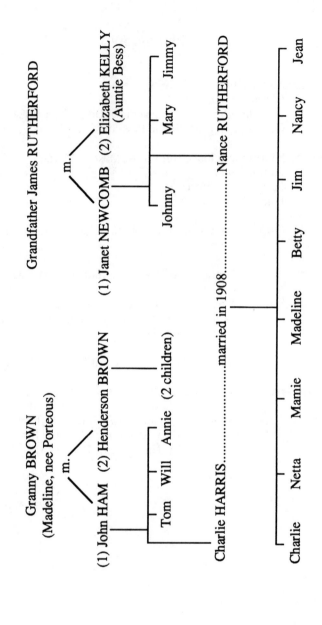

Granny BROWN
(Madeline, nee Porteous)

m.

(1) John HAM   (2) Henderson BROWN

Tom   Will   Annie   (2 children)

Grandfather James RUTHERFORD

m.

(1) Janet NEWCOMB   (2) Elizabeth KELLY
(Auntie Bess)

Johnny   Mary   Jimmy

Charlie HARRIS..............married in 1908..........Nance RUTHERFORD

Charlie   Netta   Mamie   Madeline   Betty   Jim   Nancy   Jean

Contents

CHAPTER 1

Father's beginnings

My father was born in England of an English father. The shame of it! However, since he left England and moved to Scotland with his mother, his two brothers and his sister, when he was about seven years old, he soon learned the language and could easily get away with masquerading as a true Scot. He even fooled his own children who were incredulous when the truth was revealed in later years. They managed fairly successfully from that point to blot it from their consciousness. In any case, his mother was Scottish enough to make up for her son's shortcoming, and since our English grandfather died at the age of thirty-three and Granny was still very much alive, it was no trouble for us to forget about him.

My father was no great conversationalist, or perhaps he gave up hope of getting a word in edgewise by the time the male members of our family were outnumbered by the females. 'Under petticoat government', he called it. What he had to say was usually short and succinct. He told us very little about his childhood but occasionally, while we were sinfully spreading butter on our bread, or admiring our new summer sandals, he would remark how lucky we were not to have suffered poverty as he had. We gathered he wore no shoes for most of the year and wore his father's cut-down trousers at the age of seven. However, apart from a fleeting attempt to imagine him as a child, we paid scant attention to such nonsense!

It was even more difficult for us to imagine our granny as a young mother. She was no great talker either and when I knew her in her late sixties, we rather stood in awe of this severe-looking old lady to whom we delivered our mother's well thumbed *People's Friend* on a Saturday morning, receiving a halfpenny each as reward for our trouble. By then she was a widow for the second time, her children all married, and her grandchildren growing up. Dressed in what were once known as "widow's weeds", that is, in black from neck to hem, her only jewellery made of jet, with her pure white hair scraped back into a bun, she did indeed look formidable. As an elderly woman, her skin was practically unlined and in her young days she must have been very attractive. I can only build up a shadowy picture of her young life with her parents, and then with her husband and family from the documents and stray bits of information I have.

She was born in 1859 in a tenement flat in the West Port area of Edinburgh which links the districts of Fountainbridge and the Grassmarket. At that time the area was predominantly working class. Madeline's father was a coach painter so he had a comparatively reasonable wage in keeping with that status and shortly after Madeline's birth the family were able to move to a better house in Leith.

When she was fourteen, Madeline left school and was apprenticed to a mantlemaker, nowadays what we would call a dressmaker. In Victorian Britain, conditions in this area of work were rather primitive; the girls sat at long tables in poor light, hand sewing and machine stitching for long hours, starting work at 8 am and, apart from short meal breaks, working through until 7 or 8 pm. She learned her trade well and it stood her in good stead during the lean years and beyond. She was still busy making doll's clothes for the grandchildren from her second family in the thirties. When her "time" was "out", her wages went up a little and to her parents this was a valuable contribution to their finances. Madeline continued to live with her parents for some years, perfecting her trade and growing into a confident young woman with a valuable skill at her fingertips. How she met John Ham when she was twenty-five is not known. He was from Cornwall, probably working for a time in the Leith area, and since he was also a journeyman coach painter like her father, perhaps it was through this connection. The marriage took place in England.There may be some perfectly ordinary reason why they married over the border but it prompts the questions: did Madeline's parents disapprove of John? Was it a runaway marriage? Who knows?

Once married, they set up home together at 70 Phythian Street, West Derby, where my father, Charlie was born in 1885. At that time, Britain was a rich and powerful country but at my granny's level, life was a constant struggle and Madeline and John had to budget carefully just to keep out of the poorhouse. They had none of the advantages we take for granted today such as hot and cold running water, an indoor toilet and bathroom, and reliable sewage and drainage. By 1890, three more children had been born into the Ham household; Thomas, William and Annie, so Madeline's time was fully occupied. Rising early to see her husband off to work, she then had to draw water from the nearest communal standpipe and heat what she needed to do the family wash, clean the house, and cook the meals. In her spare time she made by hand all the children's clothes. Fortunately, the children were healthy which was not always so in Victorian families. They made their own entertainments by improvisation and without any sophisticated toys. They played the usual traditional street games outside, and in the evenings, Madeline or John read to them by candlelight and taught them nursery rhymes.

Their happiness was to be very shortlived. John Ham was not very robust and seemed to suffer frequent coughs and colds. During the winter of 1890, he was not at all well, with a persistent cough which plagued him night and day. He struggled out to work in the mornings in the knowledge that there would be no income for his family if he should be ill and unable to work. Madeline noticed how irritable her husband seemed; how unwilling he had become to join in the family activities and how he would wake in the night coughing and sweating. These were common enough symptoms at that time and indicative of consumption. Nowadays, if a patient with John's illness is diagnosed early enough, the infection can be treated very quickly, with drugs, and the patient would probably not even need to be absent from his work. Then, tuberculosis was considered to be a killer.

Eventually the time came when John was unable to work and he spent his days lying weakly in bed, from time to time coughing up blood, a sign of his worsening condition. There was nothing unusual in the plight of the family as that kind of illness and death were daily occurrences, but their despair can be imagined. They more than likely shielded each other from the tragic truth, struggling along day by day, fighting a losing battle.

The last six months of John's life until he died in August 1891 must have been enormously traumatic for both him and his wife.

Poor Madeline, nursing her husband through the long nights and caring for her children through the long days, she must have been in a permanent state of despair and physical exhaustion. Worst of all, she had to appeal for "Parish relief" to keep the rent paid and clothes on the children's backs.

The most popular medicine available to ease pain and induce sleep in the late nineteenth century was laudanum. It was regarded as a panacea for all ills, despite the fact it was as habit forming as valium is today and could be bought over the counter and used for various ills, including, it is said, fretful children. It seems many nursemaids administered laudanum to their young charges to ensure a quiet life for themselves and thereby many employers were deluded into thinking that they were good at their jobs. How these employers did not notice what "peely-wally wee souls" their children had become is incomprehensible. But if you were well off, all responsibility for the mundane and irksome matters of life could be passed to paid employees and if you so desired, you rarely needed to see your unfortunate children.

John's situation was certainly one where the use of laudanum was fully justified. The question of addiction was not one that needed to be addressed since he was under sentence of death anyway. The aim was simply to ease his passing. When the end came, if he was lucky, it would come quietly as a friend in the night eased by the laudanum; but if he was less fortunate, death would be heralded by a sudden dramatic rush of blood from the lungs. Either way, when he died in August 1891, Madeline must have been at the end of her tether.

Death, like marriage and birth, was very much a family affair in those days, and took place in the home among familiar surroundings and faces so that the patient did not die in the cold, clinical atmosphere of a hospital, without a comforting word or handclasp at the end. The ritual of the funeral was all part of the pattern of grief. Perhaps Madeline and John had put aside part of their income for just such an occasion. The alternative would have been a pauper's grave, and I cannot see my Scottish granny ever allowing that to happen, even if she had to pawn or sell everything she had. She personally recorded John's death at the local Registrar's office the day after he died and then made the necessary arrangements with the undertakers.

My father could tell us nothing about his father's funeral. He was only six at the time and he and his brothers and sister were very likely looked after by neighbours while the coffin was placed in the horsedrawn hearse. The horses probably sported black plumes on their heads. The mourners would be dressed in black, or if their finances were poor, they would wear a band of black cloth on the left arm. They would walk in procession behind the cortège to the cemetery and along their route, male pedestrians would stop and remove their hats as a mark of respect. After the burial service at the graveside, the mourners would return to the house for a good dram, and eat the baked meats prepared by the women, who were not expected to attend at the graveside.

When all was over and Madeline was once more in her kitchen and her children in bed, she would have had to take stock of her life and would know she faced a bleak future. With all the conventional signs of bereavement around her, dressed in the traditional black dress, shoes and stockings, it must have been the lowest point in her life. She had no income and four children to feed and clothe. In her favour, she was thirty-two years old, strong and healthy, with plenty of Scottish smeddum, and from what I remember of her, the rôle of poor, helpless, penniless widow would not suit her at all. Her children now needed her to be both father and mother to them. Her duty to her husband was in the past and she owed it to his memory to do the best she could for their children.

For a while she managed to keep the home going with part-time work, but eventually she decided to return to Scotland. So in 1892, when my father was seven years old, she travelled north and settled in a small house in Eastfield Place in Leith, and found a job cleaning in a local school. It was the kind of job traditionally filled by widows with children to support as the hours suited their particular circumstances. They could work from 6.30 in the morning until 8.30 then hurry home to see their older children off to school, leaving the rest of the day free to care for the younger children.

At this time their finances were so low that Tom and Will, my father's two younger brothers, had to be placed in the Dean Orphanage in Edinburgh. They were very unhappy there and often ran away, adding to Madeline's worries. One can imagine her distress at having to part with two of her children, but with only her contribution to keep the home going she could see no alternative. My father escaped the fate of his brothers as he had a valuable part to play in looking after Annie, the baby, in the early morning while his mother was working. When she returned home at 8.30 am he escaped to school. On this subject Dad was more communicative to us than usual and told us more than once that while he was looking after Annie, he accidentally dropped her off the sideboard! Whether he told his mother of it we never knew. Annie seemed to be none the worse. When she was a wee bit older he taught her to play "bools" at the kerbside. So he was his mother's only helper in those years until Annie started school. By that time, as well as her school cleaning, Madeline took in dressmaking work and eventually was able to release Tom and Will from the Dean Orphanage. What a great day it must have been when these two lads returned home for good!

My father's education was patchy and as brief as he could make it, but he acquired a good grasp of the three Rs. He was the oldest male in the family and shouldered responsibilities far in excess of those he should have had for his years. During the eight years of his mother's widowhood, life was by no means easy; money was scarce and it was a constant struggle to make ends meet.

Then, unexpectedly, romance entered Madeline's life when she met Henderson Brown, a widower, who worked for the railway and lived in the same street. They married in 1899 and Madeline's future seemed more secure than it had done for years. In that same year my father started a five year apprenticeship as a joiner, and so he was able for the first time to make a financial contribution to the home. On his first day as an apprentice it was raining very heavily and as he had no watertight shoes to wear, he had to go to work in a pair of his mother's. They were plain, black and lacing but nevertheless unmistakably women's shoes. One of the foremen looked Charlie up and down and riveted by the shoes, said, "Well, now I've seen everything!" I can imagine that must have cut my father to the quick as he never forgot it. In later years he was always a most fastidious dresser, immaculately clean and tidy even when dressed for work. His employers found him intelligent, quick to learn, and mature beyond his years and he took to the work as a duck takes to water. He loved the feel of various woods in his hands and of course in his day, doors, windows, skirtingboards, the lot, were made to order in the workshop.

It must have been about this time when his mother was changing her name to Brown, that my father made the decision to change the family name on behalf of himself and his two brothers and sister, from "Ham" to "Harris". For obvious reasons we have all been grateful to him ever since for taking this step. Perhaps my father had suffered a bit of leg-pulling at school because of his name; children can sometimes be so cruel. That said, why he chose the name "Harris" we never knew, but he did such a thorough job of deleting our previous name, that we were all quite old before we knew that we had been in danger of having "Ham" as our surname! In Scotland of course a change of name could be done (and still can be), simply by informing anyone interested that you wished to be known by the new name, and using the name in all dealings, legal and otherwise. As my father owned no property, had no bank account, and his wages were too small to qualify for income tax, there were fewer problems then than there are now in the same situation. So there he was at the age of fourteen a working man, earning the princely sum of 10/- (50 pence) a week taking upon himself the important decision to change the family's surname.

Madeline, now with the protection of a husband, and her first born earning, settled down again to married life, and in due course bore her new husband a son and a daughter.

In the year my father began his apprenticeship and his mother married for the second time, the Boer War broke out. Fortunately, the members of my father's and mother's families were either too young or too old to be called to the colours. Nevertheless, my father had vivid memories of that far away war, particularly the popular songs associated with it. They were part of his repertoire and consequently part of our childhood as he taught them to us as soon as we could lisp the words. We were singing "Soldiers of the Queen" and "Goodbye Dolly Gray", forty years after that war ended and yet another had begun. A particular favourite of ours was "The Baby's Name" which went:-

The baby's name was Kitchener Carrington
Methuen Kekewich White,
Cronje Plumer Powell Majuba Gatacre

Warren Colenso Kruger
Capetown Mafeking French Kimberley
Ladysmith Bobs
Fighting Mac Union Jack Lyddite
Pretoria Blobbs!

All these names were either of prominent Boer or British Generals, or South African place names where battles or sieges had taken place, with 'Union Jack' and 'Lyddite' thrown in. Lyddite, I discovered only recently, was a new kind of material used in the making of shells. It was all Greek to us but great fun to sing!

Patriotism, of course, was rife in the land. Even Queen Victoria came out of her seclusion to travel all over reviewing troops and visiting hospitals. She did not live to see the end of the war as she died in January 1901 after a reign of sixty-four years and Edward VII, having waited in the wings for almost a lifetime, succeeded to the throne. Although he was over sixty, he was still considered to be a bit of a lad and he created more interest in the royal family than there had been in a very long time. His horses, his women, his journeys abroad were followed with interest in the daily newspapers. He was admired apparently without resentment or envy, by what were then called "the lower orders". My father was a bit of a republican at heart and often said, no matter what king happened to be on the throne at the time, "Och, what does HE matter; he can only wear one shirt at a time, same as the rest of us!"

My father's "time" was "out" in 1904, when he was nineteen and he was paid off immediately. Although he was a good worker, no employer paid journeyman's wages when he could take on another apprentice for next-to-nothing. You can be sure our father told us about those hard times when he had to go out and find work in all weathers. He usually found it by sheer persistence and determination but he often had to travel long distances on his push bike.

At one place of work some of the men when they arrived early on a wet or snowy morning, had to roll themselves in the sawdust pit to rid themselves of the worst of the water. At hedge cutting time, the sharp clippings at the side of the roads sometimes meant a puncture to be mended with the aid of a cycle repair kit. At another workshop the slowest man was paid off each week. Times were hard, but my father had been brought up in a hard school and he survived. Young and optimistic as he was, life was good and not without its lighter and romantic side.

Since my mother and father both lived in the same small area and probably went to the same school, it would seem reasonable to assume that they knew each other for some time before their romance took off. It seems that Nance Rutherford's father thought a match with Charlie Harris, a mere joiner from a very poor background, was not good enough for his daughter. Undeterred, the young couple started 'walking out' together. He was a more than usually handsome young man. She was tall, slender and goodlooking. Together they made an attractive pair.

In time, they wore down her father's opposition which was probably caused by his concern that he would lose Nance, his unpaid housekeeper, as she had looked after him, her two brothers and sister, ever since the onset of her mother's final illness. Her background was very different from my father's and we must look at that before we go further.

Nance Rutherford — 1908

Grandmother Janet Newcomb
Rutherford — 1882

Charlie Harris — 1908

Grandmother Madeleine
Porteous/Ham/Brown — 1930

CHAPTER 2

Mother's Beginnings

Rutherford is a Border name and a lot of rogues they were too. Based near Jedburgh, they were one of the many sixteenth century tribes of reivers who terrorised the border between Scotland and England. Robbery, blackmail, murder, extortion, rape, pillage and arson was the normal way of life. The King appointed wardens to try and bring order to the area, and eventually, after a great many skirmishes and bloodshed over a couple of centuries, the wardens gained the upper hand and the reiver tribes gradually dispersed. A description of the characteristics of those old Rutherford reivers strikes us as curiously familiar. Suspicious, taciturn, difficult to get to know, with an ability to endure — that sounds just like a description of my grandfather Rutherford, my mother's father and also possibly of her younger brother, Jimmy, who was killed in the First World War. Some of us today exhibit one or two of those traits.

James Rutherford, my mother's father, was born in Leith in 1863. As soon as he was old enough, he followed the same occupation as his father, that of vegetable gardener, and the family lived in the corner of Leith at the Seafield end of Leith Links, next to Seafield Cemetery. In his mature years, James was a fine, sturdy looking chap with dark hair and a heavy moustache, as can be seen in a very indistinct snapshot of him. Janet Newcomb, whom he married in 1882, was born in Glasgow in 1861, the illegitimate daughter of a domestic servant. Her mother must have been a very courageous young woman as she flouted the conventions of her day and kept her child. For seven years she supported herself and her child, and then she married a widower, by the name of Newcomb.

Janet and her parents moved to Leith and rented a house at 11 Cables Wynd, an area which now, apart from its name, bears no relation to what it once was. The old, dilapidated property has been demolished to be replaced by blocks of flats, commercial buildings and open spaces.

When Janet left school, she found work in a flax mill and she was twenty-one years old when she met and married James Rutherford and set up home with him, at Easter Hermitage in the Restalrig area of Leith. The lady who became my grandmother was a strikingly beautiful young woman, with large expressive eyes, dark hair, and a trim figure. A family photograph shows her at the height of her beauty perhaps in the year of her marriage.

The young Rutherfords were delighted when Janet soon became pregnant but their hopes came to grief when she gave birth to a daughter who survived only long enough to be named after her mother. This was a sad blow, but they were reassured when Janet became pregnant again and their son, John, was born in 1884. My mother, Agnes, or Nance as she was always called, was born to them in 1886, her sister Mary in 1888, and the youngest, James, in 1890.

Things went well for the family and grandfather's fruit and vegetable business prospered, giving them a good standard of living. He was a hard worker. He had to be up very early each morning to go to the fruitmarket with his horse and cart to purchase his produce, load it up, then start on his rounds, ringing a handbell in each street he visited to let the housewives know he had arrived. At the end of the long day, he led his horse and cart back to the stables he rented, attended to the comfort of his horse, and went home for supper and bed. It was not an easy life but he was his own boss and that gave him a respected position in his community. Jimmy Rutherford was a man of some standing and authority.

Grandfather and his growing family moved several times before settling at 13 Pirniefield Place where my mother spent most of her growing years. Her upbringing was strict, as Grandfather Rutherford was rather a disciplinarian whose word was law and not to be flouted. Although as fond of his young family as any other father, he was dour and undemonstrative; tight-fisted as well, according to Mother. In fact, she often said he was at his most generous when he had had a dram or two to loosen the purse strings. He liked his whisky and although not a drunkard, he enjoyed the occasional pub crawl. His horse knew the way home so he never came to any harm, and when he was in an alcoholic haze, mother would ask him for money for a new hat or a dress. He did, she assured us, always cough up, and more important, he had forgotten all about it next morning.

Mother had a good plain Scottish education with the three Rs uppermost in the curriculum. Her handwriting was always clear and easy to read. Unlike my father's education which was patchy due to family circumstances, she had the benefit of unbroken attendance at school. In addition, her father bought her a piano and paid for her to have lessons. He must have been on a rather extended celebration to part with the cash for such extravagance!

On the domestic side, from an early age, she helped her mother with sewing, cleaning and cooking, as her mother's health declined. As the eldest girl in the family it was expected of her. The boys in the family did no housework of course. Washing dishes was not considered a fitting occupation for them. Among other skills, she learned to knit socks for her father and brothers — in my youth she always seemed to have a sock on the needles, knitting absentmindedly and turning the heel expertly without looking at the work.

In spite of her responsibilities, her childhood was a happy one. There were no summer holidays as we know them today, but they had some days off in the "Trades Week" and grandfather took his family for a jaunt with his horse and trap to Musselburgh or Joppa. These odd days, were always referred to as "a day here and there", and were more spoken of, prized, and remembered than a fortnight on the Costa Brava is now. Treats were few, but all the more valued for that. Even if the pony and trap was not available, Portobello was within walking distance, and Leith Links just across the road.

Nance's girlhood ended when she left school at fourteen to go out to work and was expected overnight to turn into a mature woman. There was no in-between stage to allow maturity to take place slowly, and young people had to behave and dress like adults to fit into the commercial world which surrounded them. The choices open to girls leaving school were fairly limited. They could go into service but I suspect Jimmy Rutherford would have thought that beneath his daughter. Servants were poorly paid, hard worked, and usually had to "live in", which meant leaving home. Nance's help to her ailing mother was too valuable for that to be considered.

Offices employed women as clerkesses and that kind of job was regarded as more prestigious than being in service as it was a "clean job". The hours were better. Using a typewriter, then quite a new invention, had a certain amount of glamour attached to it. However, mother was not attracted to it. Nor was she attracted to the life of a shop assistant; on your feet all day and subject to the whims of inconsiderate customers — it was a daunting thought. Nursing was a career exclusively for women and required special skills and a long apprenticeship. It was very demanding and needed a great deal of determination and stamina to withstand the discipline and hard physical work. It also meant living away from home, so that ruled out nursing.

Dressmaking was not seen as a means to healthy living since at this time, in spite of the miraculous Singer sewing machine, a lot of work was still done by hand, in poor light and working conditions but Nance counted herself lucky when she found an apprenticeship as a seamstress. She started her training in 1900. Her elder brother, Johnny, had already left school and worked as a clerk in an office and in a year or two, Mary, mother's younger sister, started training as a nurse. Jimmy, the youngest, joined his father in the family business as soon as he was fourteen years old.

Just when all seemed to be going well for the Rutherfords, Grandmother Rutherford's heart problem took a turn for the worse. There was no real cure. She had to rest a lot and was unable to do any housework at all. My mother was eighteen years old at this time and had to give up her work to take over the running of the house and look after the invalid, as well as looking after her father, sister and two brothers. It could not have been easy for a young girl to take on such a demanding task and grandfather could not have been an easy man to please.

Grandmother's condition gradually worsened and when she died in 1906 at the age of forty-five, Mother, already firmly thirled to her responsibilities as the family's unpaid housekeeper, had not much hope of release. In spite of that, when handsome Charlie Harris asked her to go out with him, she said "yes". In the small amount of time they had to spare for such frivolities, they queued up for the "gods" at the 'Empire' or 'Royal' to see many of the music hall turns of their day, including Harry Lauder, Hetty King, George Robey, Vesta Tilley and Nellie Wallace who were at the height of their popularity. Both my parents were naturally musical and even without the encouragement of the wireless, which had yet to be invented, they could sing many of the latest popular songs — "The Merry Widow", "Flora Dora", "Veronique", "The Belle of New York". They particularly loved Gilbert and Sullivan operas and absorbed the words and music with great enthusiasm. All their children were indoctrinated, practically from the womb, in the intricacies of these operas, for which we have been grateful ever since. Their knowledge of old music hall songs was fairly comprehensive and some grand opera came within their orbit as well.

As yet films were in their infancy and looked on as a passing curiosity, showing no sign of the huge explosion which was to take place over the next thirty years. There were no purpose-built cinemas in Leith then, so if you wanted to see a film, however primitive, you had to accept uncomfortable seating and makeshift arrangements. No doubt my parents sampled whatever was available in this new medium.

They were a well matched pair in temperament and in appearance and must have turned a few heads when they went out strolling in the summer evenings, perhaps to watch the cricket or bowling on Leith Links, or to listen to the band playing at the bandstand. On Sunday afternoons, dressed in their best, they would go out on a decorous walk together, meeting friends along the way on a similar expedition. Conventions were strict. It was not the "done thing" to walk hand-in-hand, or for the man to put his arm round the girl's waist but if the couple were "going steady", it was acceptable for the girl to put her arm through her sweetheart's thereby staking her claim on him. The man would always make sure that he walked on the outside of the pavement nearest to the traffic, to protect his partner from any splashing from passing traffic. Both of them had to be properly dressed. He would be in a suit with a white or striped shirt with a stiff detachable collar. My father wore that kind of shirt and collar for the rest of his life and never took to modern soft collared shirts. With the collar went a tie, not too vulgarly patterned, boots or shoes, a hat, gloves, and an overcoat in cold weather. All these things put together reflected your status and your "brocht-upness".

Mother would be wearing a costume consisting of a matching jacket and ankle-length skirt with a white shirtwaister blouse, high necked and frilly, a large hat and gloves, with a long coat or mantle in winter. Shoes or neat elastic-sided boots completed her outfit. You were considered to be very improperly dressed and completely shameless if you wore no hat or gloves and any kind of casual wear was frowned on. If they met friends as they walked along, my father would touch his hat or raise it in greeting and mother would smile and incline her head in a dignified way. Good manners were very important and cost nothing.

There were plenty of places for their walks. Leith Docks attracted visitors as it was a busy and interesting place, even on a Sunday. The old Martello Tower, now rather sinister looking in its lonely glory, which had been built to defend the entrance to Leith Harbour was an edifice to examine and speculate about. If the weather was fine, it was pleasant to walk to the quaint old village of Newhaven with its small harbour, or as far as Granton, and Seafield and Portobello beach were just around the corner. So also was the terminus for the trams. Horse-drawn buses had been in operation between Leith and Edinburgh since 1833 and had gradually ousted the stage coaches. The buses in their turn were superseded by horse-drawn trams and eventually Leith adopted the electric system in 1905 "before Edinburgh", as my father always said proudly. So for a penny or two the young couple could go up to Edinburgh for a look round, although they had to change trams at Pilrig because of Edinburgh's slowness to adopt the same system.

When the tram returned to its terminus at Seafield Baths, the conductor hopped out and ran round the back end of the tram to put the cable in position for the return journey; then he hopped on the tram again and swiftly ran down the centre aisle, pushing all the seat-backs over so that the seats faced in the right direction. This conjuring feat was worth lingering a minute or two at the terminus to see.

Tram cars were very popular with courting couples and my father often took us on his knee and sang to us —

Go, go, go for a ride on the tram car car,
For we all know how cosy the tops of the tram cars are.
The seats are so small, and there's not much to pay,

You sit close together and "spoon" all the way.
There's many a miss will be missis some day,
By riding on top of a car.

Yes, Leith had plenty of amusements to offer, and although
both these young people were hard working with responsibilities
beyond their years, they made full use of their leisure time.
Charlie even found time to be in the Volunteers, the equivalent
of today's Territorials. It has to be said that he was never very
enamoured of army life but he probably enjoyed the company
and comradeship of the other young men in his unit. He once told
us they were sent out in pairs on manoeuvres and for their day's
food ration, each pair had one loaf of bread and two onions!

In the year of their engagement, Charlie made a lovely jewel
box for Nance which she treasured all her life. It is an impressive
piece of work by any standards, with her initials beautifully inlaid
on the lid, lined with red plush velvet, with a compartmented,
removable tray, beaded panels on the sides and a little lock and
key. My father gave it to me some years after mother's death and I
treasure it just as much as she did.

For a while marriage must have seemed a very remote possibility to the young couple, due to Grandfather Rutherford's
opposition and Nance's responsibilities at home but Charlie was
a very determined young man and eventually parental opposition crumbled. They were married in 1908 at 13 Pirniefield
Place. There are no photographs of the event, but being a
sensible couple, it's possible that all unnecessary frills, such as
photographs and fancy clothes were dispensed with. After their
wedding they had a weekend honeymoon at Eddleston, which
they often referred to in later years. When they returned, they
moved into a rented top flat at No. 5 Pirniefield Place just down
the road from grandfather. They were lucky to have so many
relatives and friends around them and although they were not
well off, my father had a steady job, they were young, healthy,
and in love. The future could not have looked rosier.

CHAPTER 3

Marriage

Leith, in those days before it became part of Edinburgh, was a busy, bustling place. The docks, the Shore and the business areas of Bernard Street, Commercial Street and Constitution Street hummed with life. Duke Street, the Foot of the Walk and Great Junction Street supported all kinds of shops and the rather ramshackle old Kirkgate attracted plenty of customers. On Saturday nights, the shops in the Kirkgate sold off their perishable goods before closing for the day of rest on Sunday, and there was never a shortage of customers looking for bargains.

Church life played an important part in people's lives and the pews were well covered on Sundays with well dressed bottoms. My parents were regular churchgoers and over the years all their children were quite naturally drawn into church activities. Leisure time was also dominated by the church so that there was a constant stir in the church and its halls every night of the week. There were weekly mother's meetings, drama groups, concerts, and soirées, Guides, Brownies and Scouts, sales of work, whist drives and lantern lectures, as well as two church services on Sunday, Sunday School and Bible Class. Our church was St John's (East) just round the corner from Leith Police Station. It is used now as a warehouse.

After morning service and midday dinner, the accepted thing was to take a decorous afternoon walk. Everyone was in their Sunday best, of course, to impress the neighbours. Then home, to play equally decorous games in the privacy of the parlour or best room. Snakes and ladders, ludo and tiddlywinks were popular, but card games which might encourage gambling were frowned on. If there was a family piano, only hymns or psalms were played on it and no 'respectable' family allowed their children to play games in the street on that day.

As an independent burgh, Leith had its own Town Council, administration and Council Chambers. It was a self-sufficient town. There was never any need to cross the boundary at Pilrig between Leith and Edinburgh, to shop in Princes Street or "up the Bridges", as everything we needed: clothes, food, entertainment, was within walking distance of our home. The nearest shop to my parents' house was Dallas's on the corner next door to them. It was a "wee Johnny a'thing", with groceries side-by-side with candles and paraffin. Mother was friendly with Mrs Dallas as they were about the same age and in a few years, their growing families played together in the Links, or in the space in front of the cemetery gates.

Restalrig Road was the nearest shopping area of any size. There was Noble the chemist on the corner, Leask the grocer, Smith the bakers and, of course, the Co-op. In those days, Leith Provident Co-operative Society, whatever the department, was simply called "The Store". Every time you bought something there you gave the shop assistant your share number which was then written on a flimsy along with the price of your purchase. The customer got one copy; "the Store" kept the other and from time to time, they paid out a penny or two in the pound dividend on what you had spent. This little windfall must have literally saved the bacon of many a family in lean times. It could be saved up over a period if you chose but most families were eager to claim it as soon as it was due.

My father was earning £1.15/- (£1.75 pence) a week when he married and he could manage to support himself and my mother reasonably well on that. They had rent to pay each week and food and clothes to buy but grandfather being "in the business", supplied them with all the vegetables and fruit they needed. A penny bone and tuppenceworth of carrot and turnip with barley and dried peas, made an excellent pot of broth which could last them for days. We thought it was always better on the second day! Those early days then taught our mother how to feed her family in the most economical way and even when finances were good in later years, she could never abandon the economical habits she had learned then. She passed them on to us and neither have we!

These days, the Victorian building where my parents started married life looks rather impressive. For a while it looked sad and neglected from the outside. However, in 1985, its sandstone front was cleaned and restored, giving it a new lease of life. In its prominent position near the foot of Pirniefield Place, it is a pleasure to look upon now. Up until the thirties when there was an eruption of housebuilding there, this quiet corner of Leith was surrounded by nursery ground, or was in the ownership of the landowners whose large villas were dotted around the area. Some of the land originally belonged to the Earl of Moray, so the house and nursery bounded by Restalrig Road and Prospect Bank Road was named Morayfield. Not far from there was Viewforth House and Rhynd Lodge. Pirniefield House, which is still there, was just up the road from our house. At the end of Seafield Avenue was Seagrove House and its nursery and nearer to Fillyside, stood Seacote House. Of course, knowing of the existence of these big houses and their grounds was one thing but their gates were firmly closed to the likes of us. Nevertheless, their existence gave our environment a rural atmosphere which it has now lost forever.

The neighbours who shared this desirable property with us were the Laws and the Cairns and their families. In such a closeknit group, good neighbourliness was essential, particularly as there was a shared lavatory for the two upper floors. The ground floor flat had the luxury of a lavatory all to itself.

The flat, which was gas lit, consisted of a room and kitchen. There was a tiny scullery which contained a sink, although the tap produced cold water only. There was no bath. The focal point and heart of the kitchen was the large coal-fired range which was the sole source of heat for the flat. On it water for all purposes was heated. Its oven was used for baking and the open fire for cooking meals. It was a demanding taskmaster and coal had to be brought up two flights of stairs from the coal bunker outside. It had to be kept clean and black-leaded regularly and the spent ashes removed every morning and taken down to the dustbin. In return, it had to work very hard to satisfy the demands of the household. Usually a large kettle of water was suspended over the fire simmering away so that, to some extent at least, there was constant hot water. In front of the range there stood a steel fender with a beautiful openwork pattern on it. It gleamed in the firelight and to keep it bright and shining, it was polished lovingly by mother with emery paper. We moved from that house when I was two years old but that fender is still bright in my memory, probably because it was at my own low level.

When the newlyweds moved in, the simplest of furniture was all they could afford. Some was secondhand, some passed on by kind friends and relatives. Their wedding presents were of the sensible kind such as sheets, pillowcases, tablecloths and china. Anything which could be made of wood my father made himself. The kitchen table he made then served us until the family home was finally disposed of many years later. It had leaves which folded down so that it could be put back to the wall when not in use. For all I know, it may be still giving good service in some kitchen today. A few upright chairs and wooden stools, a sideboard, and, of course, a double bed in the recess completed the furnishings.

The bedroom with its small adjoining box-room was even more sparsely furnished than the kitchen. But then their bed was in the warmth of the kitchen, so at bedtime, instead of retiring to a cold bedroom, my parents could undress by the dying glow of the range and hop into bed. What could be more convenient?

There was a drying green outside, and a pulley in the kitchen for those occasions when rain prevented drying outside. A cord suspended across the mantelpiece was used to air household linen and clothes. A zinc bath was brought out and placed in front of the fire for their personal cleanliness with hot water heated on the range. It was accepted that young married couples started out with very little and gradually built up their home over a long period. If you could not afford something then you waited until you could. Buying on the "never never" had not been invented. "Debt" was a four letter word to be spoken in hushed whispers. Had they but known it, they instinctively adhered to the tenets of Samuel Smiles, the Victorian writer who advocated self-help and hard work as a means of getting on in the world

A woman's place was still very firmly in the home and a married woman did not go out to work unless forced to by the circumstance of widowhood, or the illness of her husband. The suffragette movement was very active in 1908 and it was in that year that some of the demonstrators chained themselves to the railings of 10 Downing Street in their effort to secure votes for women. I have no doubt that when this news broke in distant Leith, it gave the male population a good laugh. Women who had time to do such things must be well off indeed, would be the general opinion of the men. Mother and her contemporaries, as wives of working men, had no time to spare for such "frivolities".

Equipment which is regarded as essential and without which the modern home seems to be incomplete, was quite unknown to them. Their daily work was time-consuming hard labour.

Washing day was a weekly slog to those women without children and a daily slog to those with children. Drip-dry and creaseless man-made fibres were far in the future, although artificial silk was being used in blouses and underwear. However, the attraction of that material was its cheapness and not that it saved work on washdays. When wet, white linen and cottons were laid out on the drying green to bleach naturally over a day or two. The rest of the wash was done the hard way and without the miraculous help of detergents. Hot water heated on the range, a ridged scrubbing board, a bar of washing soap to work up a good "graith" and arms up to the elbows in soapy water were essential. Even then, with the best will in the world, disaster could strike if the "graith" fell and you had to work doubly hard to work up a new one. A fresh lot of precious hot water sometimes had to be sacrificed to get a lather going again. After that, the clothes were rinsed in clean cold water once or twice and then they were wrung out, either by hand, or with a "hand ca'ed" Acme wringer, if you were lucky enough to have one. The clothes were now ready to hang out on the green to challenge the whiteness of the neighbours' washing. Some whites such as "bairns' hippens", or more politely "babies' nappies", had to be boiled so that on wash days the kitchen became a steamy cave, heavy with the smell of dirty and clean clothes comingling with the fragrance of mince and tatties, which was the usual washday dinner. Monday was the traditional washday but it was understood that women with children had to wash more often. But woe betide the woman who had the cheek to hang out a washing on a Sunday! Her reputation would be in tatters by nightfall.

A fresh challenge was encountered on Tuesday, ironing day. Items like sheets, towels and blankets were not ironed but were put through the mangle, an essential household item, standing sturdily on its cast iron legs. That done the actual work of ironing was tackled. A flatiron was placed near the fire to heat, then tested with a brisk spit or a wet finger on its sole. If it sizzled, then it was hot enough to iron linen or cotton. While one iron was in use, another was put to heat at the fire and so the process went on until all the clothes were ironed. It is fair to say that most women achieved remarkable results by this primitive method. Gas irons came into use in the twenties, and they must have seemed a great improvement. There was still no means of regulating the heat and the same old "spit and sizzle" test had to be used. They also made a hissing noise frightening enough to daunt the timid. Compared with these, the electric iron was a huge step forward, even without the sophisticated heat controls and steam gadgets we have now. If the washing was too dry, the housewife filled a jug with water and flicked droplets onto the washing with her fingers until she considered it damp enough for the iron to do a good job.

What about an ironing board? Well, there may have been some around in those days but not in my parents' home. My father provided a board of plywood which was laid on top of the kitchen table to protect its surface, then a thick blanket was put over that and finally a clean bedsheet folded once or twice was laid on top. This had its drawbacks of course, as things such as frocks and shirts had to be ironed in the "flat" rather than in the "round". This was the era of elaborate pin-tucked and darted blouses with leg o' mutton sleeves and lacey collars and cuffs. Even children's clothes had fussy decoration, with several tucks round the hem to allow for growth. It was time-consuming but immensely satisfying to produce a pile of lovingly ironed, clean clothes to be put away in the chest of drawers.

Making meals on our open range, Mother had no means of regulating the heat and there was a great deal of skill in producing food free from a smokey flavour or in avoiding burning food. Each housewife got to know intimately the character and vagaries of her own range and the high standard of her tattie scones, girdle scones and drop scones was the measure of how much she was in control of her range using her experience and commonsense.

In most working class homes there were no carpets and the floor covering was good, hardwearing, inlaid Kirkcaldy linoleum. Tough as old boots, it could be washed and polished with Mansion Polish to a dangerous shine. Before the polish went on, the floor was well scrubbed but a woman who used a long handled floor mop was considered to be very slapdash in her work. Everyone knew that the only way to clean a linoleum floor was to get down on the hunkers and scrub with plenty of soap and water. The luxury of wall-to-wall carpeting was unknown, and the only concession to comfort was a fireside rug, sometimes home-made.

The electrical appliances we now take for granted would have seemed like bewildering miracles to the young marrieds of 1908, and of course radio and television were still years ahead. The population had scarcely adapted yet to motor vehicles and aeroplanes. Life was hard work and both partners in marriage had to fulfil a daunting programme of physical labour just to keep the rent paid, the house clean, and its occupants well fed and healthy. Food was cheap but wages were low. Income tax was 1/2d (6 pence) in the pound. National Insurance had just come into force and had to be paid for by employer and employee alike. Socialism was still a very fashionable and young movement. It was quite the thing for wealthy people to loudly profess their support for the Socialist cause while wallowing in wealth and privilege themselves. The money some of them spent on socializing rather than socialism could have supported many a family for years.

Class distinction at my parents' level was not all that noticeable. An unskilled labourer was not looked down on if he lived a "respectable" life. In other words, caring for his family, going to church regularly, taking part in community life and neither drinking nor gambling to the detriment of his ability to support his family. The description "domestic servant" was not something to be ashamed of as it appears to be now, and there was dignity and satisfaction to be gained from work well done. As for my parents, their simple aim was to bring up a family and to "better themselves". My father probably had the ambition to have his own business and be his own boss. My mother would be hoping to move to a bigger house with hot and cold running water and a bath. This hope became an urgent necessity during the next few years when their family started to arrive. Charles, their first son was born in 1909 and in 1910 their first daughter, Janet (Netta) was born, so Mother was fully occupied with children and home. She also helped to run Grandfather Rutherford's household, continuing to be his unpaid housekeeper. But busy as she was, she was content with her lot. Fortunately, she was released from her duty to her father when, at the end of March 1911 he married for the second time.

Grandfather's new wife was a widow who described herself on the marriage certificate as "Grocer". Possibly the lady's first husband had left her well provided for. In any case, grandfather very soon took over the lease of a couple of acres of the nursery off Prospect Bank Road, known as Morayfield, a move which must have needed some capital to finance it. The newlyweds moved into Morayfield House with young Jimmy, in time for the spring planting in 1911. As well as the large Victorian villa which in the future was large enough to accommodate members of the family returning from travels abroad, there were stables and outhouses on the land, and a labourer's cottage. Very soon they took on a ploughman, Tom Hardie, and he occupied the cottage, a faithful employee for many years.

Mother must have been very relieved that her father was being well looked after by his new wife and that her responsibilities as his housekeeper had ended. By the autumn of that year she was pregnant again and in March 1912, Mary (Mamie) was born and an indecently short time later, in April 1913, Madeline. Big families were usual, of course, but my poor mother now had four children born in four years. It must have been no small achievement to get through the days of washing, ironing, cooking and cleaning and fall into bed at night, only to rise early and repeat the same programme the following day. There was now a big double bed in the room in which Netta and Mamie slept together. Wee Charlie slept in the boxroom, while Madeline occupied a cot next to the bed in the kitchen recess. The house was full of the sound of children's voices, tears and laughter, and the days were full of the bustle surrounding a large growing family.

Charlie and Nance were now responsible parents who took their rôle in life very seriously and as they brought in the New Year of 1914, they had no reason to think there was anything other than peace and security in store for them.

5 Pirniefield Place, Leith.
(Photo by Alastair Horne)

Auntie Mary

Father in uniform

Uncle Jimmy

CHAPTER 4

War

The summer of 1914 was a glorious one by all accounts and with Madeline a lively toddler, as relief from her never ending housework, my mother took her little family across the road to Leith Links to enjoy the hot summer days, or walked with them along Seafield Road, pushing a "go-car" with Madeline in it, the others hanging on somewhere, either to her long skirts, or the handle of the go-car.

In the few years since their marriage there had been changes in both parents' families. My father's brother, Will, had joined the regular British Army and was stationed in Hong Kong. He sent my mother the set of fine eggshell china which she treasured all her life. It was always kept in a glass-fronted cupboard in the parlour and we were never allowed to touch it. It hardly ever saw tea, except on very special occasions. Granny Brown and Henderson Brown lived in Boothacre Cottages with the two children of their marriage and Tom and Annie from her first marriage. Tom, aged twenty-seven in that year, was a trained jeweller and Annie, twenty-four years old, was a fully fledged tailoress. Granny had also added to her family in what would seem to be a rather casual way, an orphan boy who was lame. She was fifty-five now and still not afraid of hard work with all those people to look after.

On my mother's side, everything was going well at Morayfield. In fact, the business was so well established, it was as if there had always been Rutherfords at Morayfield and it looked as if this would continue to be the case for a very long time. The taciturn head of the family and his equally taciturn son, Jimmy, worked well together and the stepmother whom everyone called Auntie Bess, was accepted into the family circle. Mary paid them flying visits from time to time. She was nursing in a hospital in

Glasgow. She brought a breath of the outside world to the small community of relatives at Pirniefield. Her stories of hospital life always had an enthralled audience. In her attractive uniform and scarlet lined navy blue cloak, she was a glamorous figure. She was a very cheerful person and was a great one for singing the popular songs of the day in her clear soprano voice. She must have been a tonic on the wards!

The eldest of that family, Johnny, had married and had two little boys. He had taken advantage of an opportunity to leave home, choosing a life of travel with his family which sometimes sent its fortunes soaring and at other times plunging rudely down to earth. When Uncle Johnny and Auntie Jean returned to Leith for an occasional visit, they were always very good to my mother and her young family. Sometimes there were picnics or theatre outings. These occasions are still remembered in our family. Auntie Jean was a very kind-hearted person and she sometimes passed on to my mother dresses and skirts which she no longer wanted. They were always expensive and of the finest quality, costing much more than my mother could ever afford. She had been a cook before she married Uncle Johnny but you would never have guessed it. She had the air of being a real lady and was accepted as such wherever she went. She had the most unusual and memorable voice I have ever heard. It was soft and muffled. I can still hear it in my mind's ear and her musical laugh.

When speaking of how Uncle Johnny made his money, Mother and Dad always looked very mysterious and somehow disapproving, giving the impression that there was something not quite respectable about it. I think now that there was nothing shady about it at all and that he made his money by speculation and investment on the advice of influential employers and friends. Of course, according to my parents' views, if you did not actually do physical work and dirty your hands to earn money, then it must be disreputable. I have no memories of him at all but a funny story about him survives which has been told and re-told over the years. It seems he and Auntie Jean had a rather smelly old dog which died of natural causes and which was buried in the back garden. Several years later they were moving house and Johnny insisted on digging up the body, now partly decomposed and even smellier, and moving it with them!

In the middle of the idyllic summer of 1914, Britain declared war on Germany for reasons so often considered elsewhere that I need not tax my brain by exploring them here. Even in far off Scotland, the excitement at such an event was noticeable. Caught up in war fever, young men from all over Scotland queued at recruiting stations to enlist, train and take part in the first actions of the war, alongside the regular British Army and the Territorial Army.

As my mother took her little brood out for walks that August, she must have felt that the news of war was not half so important as her own knowledge that another little Harris was on the way and due in March 1915. No doubt her head was full of questions about how on earth she could cope with another baby in such cramped conditions, let alone feed her large family. Now there was the added worry that her husband might be conscripted into the army or some other form of service.

Still, she would console herself, everyone said that the war would be over by Christmas. Of course it would! Everyone knew we could lick the Germans within a few months and send them packing back to their own country. After all, the British Army had been handling that sort of thing all over the world for many years and this would be no different. However, that attitude soon evaporated and it became clear to all that Britain was committed to a long, bitter war and that more volunteers or conscripts would be needed to reinforce the Regular and Territorial armies.

The brutal truth was that men were being killed in the battlefields of France faster than they could be replaced by trained men. A nation-wide appeal for volunteers was launched. A poster was published and distributed throughout Britain calculated to encourage patriotism and an irresistible desire to join the fighting forces.

A CALL TO ARMS

An addition of 100,000 men to His Majesty's Regular Army is immediately necessary in the present National Emergency.

Lord Kitchener is confident that his appeal will be at once responded to by all those who have the safety of our Empire at heart.

TERMS OF SERVICE

General Service for a period of 3 years or until the war is concluded.
Age of Enlistment between 19 and 30.

HOW TO JOIN

Full information can be obtained at any Post Office in the Kingdom
or at any Military Depot.

GOD SAVE THE KING!

In a huge demonstration of patriotism, men from all walks of life
and of all ages, rushed to the recruiting stations to volunteer.
Lads as young as fifteen years lied about their age and older men
knocked off a few years from their true age, so that they could be
accepted. Great pressure was put on any reluctant heroes by the
newspapers. Sometimes the men were "got at" by their wives or
sweethearts, encouraged by crude appeals such as "Is your best
boy wearing khaki?", or "When the war is over and your husband
is asked 'what did you do in the War?', is he to hang his head
because YOU would not let him go?" It took almost as much
courage to withstand such open criticism and pressure as it would
to be in the front line.

Conscription was expected to follow and unmarried men would
be the first to go. My father, as an old man of twenty-nine,
married, with four children and another on the way, should have
been well down the list of conscription. Moreover, he had had a
taste of army life while in the Volunteers and was not anxious to
repeat the experience.

He always told us he "wouldn't have his dog in the army" but
he came to the conclusion that if he waited to be conscripted, he
would have no choice about the service he was to be drafted into
and would probably end up in the P.B.I. (poor bloody infantry).
So he decided to volunteer and chose the Royal Engineers in the
hope that he would be able to use the skills he had developed
in peacetime. Off he went to war, leaving my mother to manage
her family on the strength of a soldier's family allowance. It was

understood that as a married man with children he would not be posted overseas but due to a mix-up, he found himself at the station about to entrain for France. Fortunately for him, the mistake was discovered and he was taken off the draft in the nick of time.

My father's army career is shrouded in mystery, mainly because when he was demobilised in 1918, he was only too glad to leave that period of his life firmly in the past. He seldom talked about it but we gained the impression that he did not enjoy army life. His one ambition throughout the war was to get home to his wife and family. In spite of himself, however, he was promoted to corporal and then to sergeant. Towards the end of the war he was reduced to the ranks for some heinous crime or other. Not, I hasten to say, on charges of drunk or disorderly conduct, or being absent without leave but probably because of his tendency to challenge any order if he thought it unreasonable. He was always very smartly turned out and his innate sense of pride in his appearance happened to be just what the army wanted to foster. He was stationed for most of his service days in Sandwich in Kent. He seems to have liked it there and apart from the occasion when he escaped the overseas draft, Dad's war was reasonably peaceful and comfortable, compared with others.

Of the other eligible men in my parents' family circle, Will, already in the regular army, immediately found himself pressed into service in France. Tom is a rather shadowy figure and no one in the family now remembers if he served during the war. Johnny and his family seem to have been abroad during the war years and so he could not be called to the colours. Mary, of course, as a nurse, suddenly became much in demand and was busier than ever, looking after the war wounded who very soon began to pour into Britain from the battlefields of France.

Mother's younger brother, Jimmy Rutherford, was twenty-four years old when war broke out, strong and healthy from his outdoor life at his father's nursery garden. He was unmarried, which made him especially eligible for service. At first, before the urgent call came for volunteers, Jimmy said to his father, "I'll join up when the neeps are in", so that his father would have his assistance with that job before winter came. However, with war fever at its height and all his friends hastening into uniform, like sheep to the slaughterhouse, the neeps had to be forgotten and

Jimmy went off to Aldershot to join the 8th (Service) Battalion of the Black Watch to train for service in France.

Training for these green volunteers was very tough indeed and the weaklings were soon ruthlessly weeded out and posted to less difficult duties. In the early days, the issue of uniforms and equipment was slow and there was some jocular rivalry among the companies as to which was the best equipped.

A typical day for these men began at 6 am with an hour's marching, running and exercise before breakfast. After breakfast, they usually marched several miles to a battle training area, returning in time for tea and then lectures were given. It was a very hard, disciplined life but Jimmy felt fit and had no trouble fulfilling the work expected of him.

In January 1915, the fully equipped and trained men were inspected on Laffan's Plain by Lord Kitchener. This parade took place in a downpour of rain in which the troops waited for several hours, their heavy uniforms becoming sodden and uncomfortable. The cold must have penetrated to their very bones. It took days to dry out their clothes and equipment. No doubt this was thought to be good training for trench warfare and it was.

The Battalion landed at Bologne early in May and marched to Arques where they were billeted for a few days. They could hear quite plainly the sound of the guns from Ypres. What were the thoughts of those young men when they heard the noise of battle so clearly for the first time? Excited anticipation perhaps? Enthusiasm for the coming battles? Thoughts of home and loved ones? They soon faced the reality of war. That summer the 8th fought in various sectors of the front and lost some of their number but for a few days at the end of August, they rested and had a pleasant time in country surroundings at Robecq. They returned to the line early in September in preparation for the battle of Loos.

At home, Jimmy's family knew that his training was completed and that he would soon be in the fighting line. His letters told them very little and sometimes all they got was a Field Service Post Card with various statements on it. The soldier deleted what was inappropriate. This is how it looked:-

I am quite well.
I have been admitted into hospital

    (sick   (and am going on well.
    (wounded   (and hope to be discharged soon.

I am being sent down to the base.

I have received your   (letter dated ....
                          (telegram ....
                          (parcel dated ....

Letter follows at first opportunity.
I have received no letter from you

                          (lately.
                          (for a long time.
Signature only ....

Date ....

It was enough to let the family know that their boy was still alive.

My mother, in her letters to Jimmy, was able to tell him of the birth in March of another daughter, Elizabeth (Betty) and of how a few weeks after her birth, she gave the family a scare, falling gravely ill with glandular trouble. Dad had to get compassionate leave to come home and things looked very bad for a while. Betty, however, was made of stern stuff and surprised everyone by fighting her way back to health. In later years, when Mother told Betty about this illness, she said it had been touch and go but "You had mair ill tae dae, Betty!"

Jimmy's letters home had to be few and far between. They were preparing for what proved to be one of the bloodiest battles of that dreadful war. The battle of Loos in September 1915 was one in which the British used poison gas and while the troops stocked the trenches with gas cylinders and ammunition, a four day field artillery bombardment of the enemy trenches was in progress. The battalion was placed opposite the Hohenzollern Redoubt, a salient projecting from the enemy lines. The eve of the battle was spent packed in reserve trenches trying to sleep and keep warm in the chilly autumn night. This was their first taste of a planned offensive. Early on the morning of 25th September the men took their places and awaited their orders while gas was released. The wind carried it towards the enemy lines, and at 6.30 am the attack began. They were under withering machine gun fire and lost a great many men but by 7 am the Redoubt was taken and the battalion pressed on to take the main German trench.

The next few days were crucial. In fact the enemy began to regain hard fought ground. The situation was desperate. Then Lieutenant Colonel Cameron of Lochiel with a force of seventy Black Watch and thirty Cameron Highlanders advanced to the Redoubt. Perhaps Jimmy was one of the Black Watch group as he was an experienced man who could be trusted to use his initiative and lead other men. About 3 pm when the whistle blew, they went over the top, kilts flying, faces dirty and determined. They went into battle in the face of fierce resistance and they suffered many losses but the Redoubt was secure. During this intense action they were left without any trained bombers and impromptu classes on how to light and throw grenades had to be improvised in the rear trenches. The battle was won but the battalion had lost nineteen officers and four hundred and ninety-two other ranks in the three days of fighting.

The simple, bare account of this action in the regimental histories cannot possibly convey what these young men experienced in a very short and traumatic space of time when they saw friends with whom they had trained, laughed and joked struck down beside them. It defeats the imagination and it would be a presumption to try and analyse their feelings in such circumstances.

The survivors withdrew to Béthune to rest and clean up. The 8th was now weak in numbers. Many valuable and experienced officers and men had been lost. But they were back in the line at Ypres early in October, sometimes in appalling wet conditions. Often the men had to stand knee deep in liquid mud. During that month they lost another twenty-six men.

CHAPTER 5

Jimmy's War

In the middle of December 1915, Jimmy's battalion was in Ballieul to rest and train for the next tour of duty. There the men spent their first Christmas in the army. What was it like? Did they observe the long standing tradition in the British Army that at Christmas dinner the officers and NCOs serve the men at table? Did they enjoy an off duty atmosphere of camaraderie; drinking and eating together, exchanging bawdy jokes and army songs? Did they drink to forgetfulness after what they had seen and done in the battlefield? Was a toast drunk to absent, maimed, and dead friends? Whatever it was like, they must have been well aware that this might be the last Christmas for some of them.

It was perhaps during this first break in the fighting that Jimmy, now a sergeant, came home on leave, arriving in Leith in his battle-stained kilt and jacket, his kitbag slung over his shoulder. His father made him stand at the door of Morayfield House and strip off all his clothes so that they could be fumigated in the oven to rid them of vermin. What changes did his family see in him? The photograph of him taken at this time and which in our childhood looked down on us from the sideboard, shows a man who looks much older than his twenty-five years. He regards us with a steady gaze, a stocky, sturdy man with dark hair and the fashionable heavy moustache of that day, dressed in his buttoned up army jacket and broad webbing belt. On that first leave the family found he was the same Jimmy but more quiet and withdrawn. He told them nothing of his life in the trenches, except the cheerful things they wanted to hear.

He spent his leave working with his father in the nursery, preparing the ground for the growing season to come. My mother had her new baby to show off to her brother and he often sat in her kitchen toasting his toes at the fire, dandling the baby while she got on with her work. Even to his sister, Jimmy's thoughts about the hell he had left behind and to which he must return, would forever remain unspoken. How could he explain that to him life and death in the trenches represented reality and life at home a dream? The family saw him go back to France without tears, in the good old Scottish way.

Jimmy rejoined the battalion in January 1916. There was a new intake of raw recruits, and training, especially in the use of hand grenades, was intensified. He was a seasoned veteran now and a valuable leader of inexperienced men. His calm, solid unruffled manner was an encouragement to nervous and less confident men. After all, he had seen plenty of trench warfare and he had survived the Battle of Loos unscathed. Young as he was, he represented a father figure. He no doubt accepted his rôle willingly and gave help and support when it was needed during the battalion's front line action at the end of that month. In May, news came that they were under orders for the Somme. On the long march to the battlefield, Jimmy's twenty-sixth birthday came and went, probably unnoticed by him but at home, the thoughts of his father and sisters were with him on that day. But how could they, in their douce wee corner of Scotland, possibly imagine what Jimmy's daily life was like? It was as well for them that they could not, otherwise their lives would have become intolerable at the thought of the true horrors of that war.

Fortunately for Jimmy, his unit took no part in the first days of the Battle of the Somme, days of carnage unparalleled either before or since. Hardly any books were published about it after the war. Writers and publishers alike just wanted to forget it. Only after the Second World War when so many books were written about that, did the books about Loos, the Somme, Ypres and Vimy Ridge begin to appear.

The battle began for the "poor bloody infantry" at 7.30 am on the first day of July. The horrors of that first day come back to haunt all of us in books and poetry. It has become even more vivid now that we can sit at home and watch on our television sets some of the survivors talking quietly and calmly about that day. The tears spring to our eyes as these old men talk of the friends they lost in the mud and blood of the Somme. "A useless slaughter of men", they say. "The 'top Brass' should have been shot", they say. "We never stood a chance", they say. Most of them say that there has not been a day since that first day that they have not been haunted by what they saw.

8th Battalion was soon pressed into action in the battle. Their orders were to capture the village of Longueval. Three o'clock in the morning of the 14th of July found them in position on the slopes near the village. Their morale was high and there were jokes and laughter as they prepared their weapons and equipment. They began the advance at 3.25 am. Resistance from the Germans was bitter and bloody. It was 5 o'clock in the afternoon before all that day's objectives had been won. By that time all four company commanders were either killed or wounded. At nightfall the survivors, still under shellfire, fell asleep exhausted, some still on their feet. The stretcher bearers retrieved the dead and wounded as best they could under fire, and worked far into the following morning, attending to the walking wounded. The more severely wounded had to be taken to the field stations behind the lines where doctors worked under great pressure. The next day or two brought very little progress. One night, explosives and gas shells trapped the battalion's transport and ration parties, injuring and killing men and horses. Vital supplies of food and ammunition were jeopardised. In spite of that, in spite of their reduced numbers and in spite of continual bombardment from the enemy lines, a strong attack was launched in the afternoon of the 18th, and eventually the enemy was driven out of the greater part of Longueval.

Very early the following morning the 8th was withdrawn to Carnoy. Their strength was reduced to six officers and one hundred and sixty-five other ranks and as roll calls were taken, the survivors noted without comment the gaps in their numbers but must have breathed an involuntary sigh of relief that they themselves were alive. Wearily, they cleaned their guns and equipment, and spent the rest of the day relaxing.

In my childhood a framed picture hung on our living room wall — it was entitled, "Resting after the Battle of Longueval". It showed some kilted soldiers standing or reclining on the ground, drinking mugs of what we assumed was tea. The soldiers looked very tidy and clean. I suppose that picture represented the whole First World War for us. That and the photograph of Uncle Jimmy. I realise now that this was a posed photograph for the people at home. There is a photograph in the regimental history of the Black Watch showing soldiers relaxing after that battle. It shows a more realistic scene. The men are standing in line for their rum ration, holding out their mugs for the sergeant to dole it out. So it was not tea as we had thought! They look into the camera with muddy faced grins. Some are wearing tin hats, some the tam o'shanter, others are in service caps, in tunic and trousers, and some are kilted with the khaki apron which they wore over the kilt in battle so that their regiment could not be identified. To the Germans they were known as the "Ladies from Hell" and their reputation as fearsome fighters, determined and courageous, was formidable. This group of dirty, variously garbed tatterdemalions, who have just fought a tough action to gain a few yards of foreign land, command our respect as well as our pity. They have lost many of their friends and officers in a bloody battle but there they stand, quaffing their rum ration and smiling cheekily at the camera as if they had just had a rather rough game of football. Jimmy, although not in the photograph, must have been somewhere near doling out the rum ration to his own men, with as stout a heart as any for the battles still to be fought and won.

A period of calm and rest for the 8th followed the battle at Longueval while they received a fresh intake of officers and men to replace their dead and wounded. They were fully occupied once more in training and re-organisation. The weather was fine and they soon recovered their spirits and efficiency.

Towards the end of September they were under orders for a second tour of the Somme battle area. The object this time was to attack and capture the Butte de Warlencourt and the trench system surrounding it. They were in reserve, bivouacked in High Wood in the old German trenches and subjected to the constant din of battle for several days. They took over the Flers line from a detachment of Seaforths and Argylls and spent four days clearing the battlefield under fire and burying the dead. On 17th October, they were in action and captured new ground. The next day or two brought bitter fighting to defend their positions but by 5 o'clock on the evening of the 19th, the battle was won. The Germans were finally beaten off and the men were jubilant.

Torrential rain had fallen throughout that day and the trenches were practically impassable. Amidst the confusion of sporadic action, the stretcher bearers worked to bring in the wounded and load up the ambulances. Tired as they were, Jimmy and his men gave assistance, where they could. It was while this work was going on, and in the muddy, bloody, euphoric aftermath of the battle, that he was killed by a shell at about 5.30 pm. His war was over.

The surviving members of the 8th were pulled out of the line and retired to High Wood next morning. The state of the ground was such that many platoons took eight hours to cover the four miles between the trenches and High Wood. Two hundred officers and men were missing, dead, or wounded.

News of this battle and its outcome quickly arrived in a Britain already bowed down with the sorrow of the disastrous casualties of the previous three months. By this time there was hardly a street in Britain without some drawn blinds and families dressed in mourning black. To the ordinary people of Britain, the sight of men recovering from wounds or amputations was a familiar one by now. Even without that reminder, the newspapers published casualty lists daily, and although the next of kin were informed by telegram from the War Office, people scanned those lists for news of friends and relatives. There were various headings to be studied such as, "Died of wounds", "Wounded", "Missing", "Missing believed killed", "Suffering from Gas Poisoning", or "Believed to be a prisoner in enemy hands". None made cheering news. Readers of these lists eventually developed a sort of hardened attitude which protected them from too much grief. It was not that they were callous or unfeeling but simply that there was a limit to the emotional impact made by daily reading of such lists.

The Rutherfords probably scanned these lists from time to time but they would be well aware that if anything happened to Jimmy, his father would be informed by telegram from the War Office. Like so many other families, they lived in fear of the sight of a telegraph boy in his distinctive uniform approaching the house. When that fear became cold reality, they were devastated. Our Auntie Mary came to our house to break the news to my mother that Jimmy had been killed in action. They wept together and comforted each other as best they could. The thought that they would never again see their young brother was hard to grasp. The thought that he might have suffered terrible wounds before he died tortured them. Mercifully, their imaginations were unable to visualise the true circumstances of Jimmy's death in the mud and blood of the trenches. Only one who had seen such sights could .

The family observed the conventional period of mourning, at that time, a year. They dressed entirely in black, or wore a black band on the left arm. My father wore one black button on his uniform tunic to show he had lost a near relative in the war.

The Rutherfords may have derived some comfort from the letter Jimmy's Company Commander, Captain Murray, wrote to his father.

France, 26th October 1916.

Dear Mr Rutherford,

It is with very real regret that I write to sympathise with you over the death in action of your son.

We were holding a line which had just been won, and he was killed instantaneously by a shell about 5.30 pm.

In your son, Mr Rutherford, I feel I have lost a personal friend. He was a Lance-Corporal in my Platoon (13 Platoon) in the old days at Borden, and when we first went out to France. As a Lance-Corporal he was always smart, efficient, and above all, cheery. The spirits of the Platoon never flagged when Rutherford was near. I lost touch with him, after the battle of Loos, where I was wounded and sent home. Two months ago, however, I rejoined the regiment to find your son a Sergeant (Platoon Sergeant of No. 15). He was the same efficient, cheery Rutherford of old but lately he confessed that his nerves were not what they had been (like the rest of us), and that he was tired of the war.

He has died, and we have lost a true staunch friend and a fine soldier, and everyone who knew him feels the shock of his loss. But he died for his country with clean heart and clear conscience, and you should be proud of him.

Yours sincerely,

R.N.M. Murray, Capt.

O.C. D. Coy., 8th B.W.

Poor Captain Murray must have had to write many such letters, always worded to give the impression that death was instantaneous, to spare the relatives from the anguish of imagining their loved ones in terrible pain from their dreadful wounds. The Rutherford family's imagination shied away from such details, although I believe that a returning comrade of Jimmy's visited them while on leave and said Jimmy's "head had been blown off", which sounded quick and clean.

The letter from Jimmy's CO was read by the Harris children hundreds of times, even although the older ones could not remember him and the younger ones were born after his death. As the years went by and we were eventually involved in our own terrible war, we began to feel some affinity for this poor man cut down in his youth. Our yearly involvement at school on Armistice Day, the 11th of November was also a reminder. To us, who have now inexplicably grown old enough to be his mother or father, Jimmy can never grow any older.

8th Battalion went on to further battles and Captain Murray was awarded the Military Cross. On 14th November the long, wasteful, Battle of the Somme ended. It was eight months before the dead could be cleared from no-man's land. Identification was often impossible due to the appalling conditions in which these men had fought and died. It could not have been a pleasant task to try and retrieve paybooks and identification from bodies, or parts of bodies which had lain in the open for some time. The cleaning up parties were often working under enemy shellfire or machine gun fire. If there was time and opportunity, a grave large enough to accommodate six bodies head to foot was hastily dug and filled in. Sometimes they were merely tipped into the nearest shell hole which was then filled in. As Jimmy is listed as having "no known grave", he must have been unidentifiable and his name appears among 73,000 others on the Thiepval Memorial where once stood the village of that name. Destroyed during the fighting, it was never rebuilt.

To acknowledge his death in some way in the absence of his remains, his father had his name, rank and regiment added to the gravestone in Seafield Cemetery which already covered the grave of his first wife, Jimmy's mother.

In the thirties, we found our own way of reminding ourselves of the uncle who had died before we were born. Each time we visited Edinburgh Castle, we went to the Shrine and looked his name up in the huge books in which the names of the dead of the Great War are listed.

Group — Father, Mother, Netta, Charlie, Betty, Madeline, Mamie.

CHAPTER 6

Keeping the home fires burning

In war time Britain, the population was learning the art of survival in a hard world. Food became scarce; submarine attacks on our merchant shipping had caused serious shortages. Eventually, the Government had to ask the people to make do with less food, particularly bread. The women took these hardships in their stride, waiting in line patiently for margarine, fruit, or fish, with which to feed their families. Thus the tribal rite of queuing, based on the principle of fair play, took hold and remains with us today. Other nationalities fail to understand it. They think it is a peculiarly British characteristic. The Rutherfords and the Harrises were lucky to have fruit and vegetables available without queuing, through Grandfather Rutherford's business.

On the whole, my mother managed to keep the family healthy in war time. However, some time in 1917, our Charlie, then eight years old, fell seriously ill with diphtheria and he had to go into the City Hospital for a few anxious weeks. The hospital bulletins in the *Edinburgh Evening News* were eagerly studied each night. It was many more weeks before he was released and sent home. After that, his strength had to be built up slowly until he could walk and run again. This illness of Charlie's had a strange repercussion in later years, as it turned out that the girl he married had been in the City Hospital at the same time, with the same illness. Quite a coincidence.

Fuel was in short supply and rationing was introduced in 1917. So many coalmen had been called up by that time that householders had to fetch their own supplies from the coal depots. The women, my mother among them, wheeled an old pram or makeshift barrow to the coalyard to collect their ration of coal to feed the voracious appetite of the kitchen range.

Although short of food and other things, and if life was not exactly comfortable in war time Leith, at least people felt safe there. Snug and smug in far off Scotland, they felt the Germans would not bother with such an unimportant part of the British Isles. Yes, they had read about the Zeppelin raids on England. This time it was a positive advantage to be not worthy of attention. Let the English get on with it!

The Germans had been sending over Zeppelins since the beginning of 1915 on rather haphazard bombing missions. For one thing their aircraft were not equipped with sophisticated navigational aids — their pilots had to wait for a bright moonlight night, cruise around the British Isles looking for the correct target, then drop bombs where they thought they were likely to cause the most damage. It was completely against the Rules of War laid down by the Hague Convention which stated that "war should not be waged in any circumstances on civilians". However, civilians killed and injured in the war numbered about 4,000. London was the usual target for the Zeppelin raids and a complete blackout was in force there but there was no difficulty in identifying the Thames gleaming in the moonlight. Secure in the knowledge that the British had no aircraft which could intercept them, and no effective anti-aircraft guns on the ground either, bombs were dropped in an almost leisurely and casual manner.

Lulled into a pleasant feeling of security, the folk in Edinburgh and Leith were astounded when, one night in April 1916, after a lovely spring day, out of a clear starry blue sky, the destruction of war was visited on them. They say that the Zeppelins were looking for the Forth Bridge and Rosyth, or Edinburgh Castle where many soldiers were billeted. It was said that they were after the whisky stores in Leith. Reports conflicted a great deal.

The attack threw the general population into a panic. They had no instructions from the Government as to how to cope with the situation, or how to protect themselves. The noise and flash of exploding bombs, the glare of fires, the cries of people running for safety tore the beautiful springtime sky apart.

My mother took her children round to Granny Brown's house, more for company than for safety. There they huddled together, trembling and fearful until the raid was over. Grandfather Rutherford invented his own measures on the spur of the moment and in his panic said, "Yoke the horses, we'll gang to Glesca", although why he felt it to be safer in Glasgow is a mystery. I expect someone reminded him that a journey like that with horses would take many hours. He probably settled for a stiff whisky instead. Strangely, although you would think this occasion would be a memorable one, none of the older children of our family have any detailed memories of it. They remember seeing the Zeppelin but not the noise of the bombs.

The amount of damage done was revealed next day. Many working class homes had been hit, thirteen people killed and twenty-four injured. It must have been a traumatic experience for the folk of Edinburgh and Leith to realise just how vulnerable they were. For many nights after that raid, they retired to bed fully clothed in order to be ready for anything.

As the development of air defence and anti-aircraft guns improved, the Zeppelin threat diminished but a great many young men, German and British, were to lose their lives in the air in those war years.

In May 1915 there occurred a disaster which stunned all Scotland with grief and pain. A troop train carrying Scottish troops was in collision with other trains at Gretna Junction, eight miles north of Carlisle. Five hundred men of the 7th Battalion Royal Scots left Larbert at 3.25 am on Saturday the 22nd and a little before 7 am, their train collided with a passenger train. Then the London to Glasgow Express and a goods train ploughed into them. Fire broke out immediately and there were many casualties, including some women and children who had been in the passenger trains.

The dreadful news broke over Leith by word of mouth first of all. Then the story was in the evening newspapers. Dalmeny Street Drill Hall was the battalion headquarters of 7th Royal Scots, so most of the men involved belonged to Edinburgh and Leith. On the Sunday evening, the bodies were brought to the hall for identification by relatives.

The funerals took place on the Monday afternoon departing from the Drill Hall to go to Rosebank Cemetery. All traffic along the route was stopped. Thousands stood in silence as each coffin covered by a Union Jack, was brought out and put into the Red Cross motorised waggons which were used as hearses. As the cortège moved slowly off, the band of the Argylls played slow music with muffled drums.

At Rosebank, forty-eight coffins were lowered into the trench which had been dug for them. These were the unidentifiable dead. It was well into the evening by the time the coffins of the identified men arrived. When all was finished, a firing party played their part and the Last Post was sounded.

Leith citizens who witnessed these funerals never forgot the impression it made on them. My mother and father spoke of it from time to time over the years, so we were in no doubt about the impact it had made. It seemed so unfair that soldiers, perhaps on their way to the battlefields of France, should be killed in such a way with no chance to defend themselves against their unseen enemy.

A disaster of wider effect overtook Britain in the spring of 1918. An epidemic of Spanish influenza broke out at Scapa Flow and gradually spread throughout the country. Hardly a family was spared. The 'flu could strike and kill within twenty-four hours. Whether by luck, or our mother's care of us, our family was spared the distress of this illness. Gradually the 'flu infection weakened and faded.

In March 1918, the Germans launched an offensive in a last desperate attempt to destroy the British Army. In three weeks they regained ground which had taken six months of hard fighting to gain. Our troops suffered tremendous losses. Morale was not at its highest but they defended their positions and eventually the tide of war turned and they began to advance. Villages which had been occupied by the Germans for three years were liberated. During that summer the Germans began to retreat and the Allies were within sight of victory. The Armistice was signed in November. A large number of Britain's men had been sacrificed.

Soon my father was released from the army. He came joyfully home to his young wife and family, climbing the two flights of stairs to come into the welcoming glow and warmth of the range in the small kitchen of the flat in Pirniefield Place. Smart as always in his uniform which he would soon gratefully discard, he unpacked his kitbag at the kitchen table. Then he handed out the presents he had brought home for each child. Betty still remembers that he had a doll for her but that it was not very cuddly as it was made of wood! Ungrateful child!

What a night that must have been. For the first time in four years, plans could be made for the future. Even the fact that my father had no job and would have to start searching for work the very next day, could not lessen the relief and joy that was felt. They had survived. That was enough. His children have only the vaguest memories of that winter evening when my father came home from the war but I'm sure my parents never forgot it. When the children were all asleep, Netta, Mamie and Madeline in the big double bed in the bedroom, Betty in her cot, and Charlie in the wee boxroom bed, the parents talked far into the night of their plans and hopes for the future.

The next day brought the cold realities of life to their attention when my father set out to find employment. Leith slowly began to return to some sort of normality. Things could never be the same as before, of course. There were too many reminders of the war all around us. There were ex-servicemen damaged in body or in mind, feebly playing musical instruments in the streets to earn a few coppers, or just begging. In my own young schooldays long after the end of that war, I remember a poor soul who had been "shell-shocked" in the trenches who used to march about in his ragged, dirty clothes shouting military orders. There was an absent look in his eyes. His experiences in battle completely blotted out every other experience in his life. We saw many men in those days minus an arm, a leg or a mind who had been sacrificed in the service of their country. Had it been worth it? To the ordinary people of Britain the answer then, and later, was 'no'.

Britain had won the Great War but were just as beaten as the Germans at the end of it. Where were the leaders of men who might have become Members of Parliament, Cabinet Ministers, business executives and leaders of communities? Dead in the trenches. Where were all the university graduates to teach a younger generation, or become captains of industry? They went straight from university into uniform, then to the battlefields of France.

Women's rôle in the post-war world changed too, possibly for the better. They had proved that, as well as being capable of the work of servants, shop girls, dressmakers, wives and mothers, they could also work in munitions factories doing a man's job. They could drive ambulances at the front. They could nurse the wounded and dying in battle conditions and many more jobs. By the end of the war there were postwomen, coalwomen and even women chimney sweeps! Their efforts won them a modest success for women's suffrage as at the end of the war a Bill was passed granting women over thirty years old the vote. This was a step in the right direction but if women had the delusion that they were on their way to being on an equal footing with men, they were wide of the mark. That is still a long running and never ending story.

The lives of the rich had also been changed. They had lost many of their promising young men. Not only that, many of their servants went off to war and never returned. Those who came back hale in mind and body no longer wanted a life in service. After all, the Government had promised them "a land fit for heroes to live in" and heroes did not become servants. As a result of this attitude, the number of servants employed in large houses dropped. In fact, they disappeared altogether in more modest homes. So the great ladies had to put coal on the fires themselves instead of ringing for a footman, or open a window or door without help. These women, who previously had received assistance when getting dressed, now had to do so without a maid and manage by themselves. Garments once difficult to fasten, with masses of tiny buttons and whalebone stays, dangerously tight and impossible to manage alone, soon disappeared. As a result, a much more natural look in women's clothes developed. The decline of the servant class continued for many years until, after the Second World War, the word "servant" almost fell into disuse.

Among the working classes, the category into which my family fitted, their antidote to war was work, if they could find it. No special consideration was given officially to ex-servicemen. A kind hearted employer, probably himself a returned serviceman, might favour an old soldier or sailor. My father had too much pride to stoop to such shifts to get a job, even although he considered that four years of his life had been recklessly squandered to no good purpose. It would have been understandable if he had felt he was now owed a living. That was not his way however, and he travelled miles on his bicycle in all weathers whenever there was a prospect of work. He rose from his bed in the early morning to be on time and returned home late in the evening to his family.

But in spite of the still lingering discomforts of post-war living, that first Christmas and New Year after the war were very special for the Harrises. Even the Rutherfords must have celebrated.

Jimmy's death was two years in the past now. Perhaps my father and mother relaxed their teetotal rule and there was laughter and singing, fun and games and general rejoicing. Of course, Christmas Day was an ordinary working day in Scotland but New Year's Day was a general holiday for all. After that, it was back to "parritch an'auld claes" on the second day of the new year. The desperate days of war were behind them and the year 1919 was welcomed with great enthusiasm and hope.

Group — Netta, Betty, Charlie, Madeline, Mamie.

CHAPTER 7

Family matters

My parents settled down to married life again with their five children. My father found a job which suited him with a man who had his own joinery business in Musselburgh. They worked well together and mutual respect developed between them. We came to know Mr Currie and his wife as they were invited to our house occasionally. Unusually for that time, they were vegetarians which we carnivores thought a bit eccentric, but we liked them.

My parents probably considered their family was complete now. My father was 33 and my mother 32, practically middle-aged! And what a fine family those first five Harrises make as we can see from a photograph of them taken in 1916 to send to my father when he was away in the army.

The eldest, Charlie, at seven years old was a very solemn little boy. Outnumbered by his sisters, he was inclined only to speak when he had something to say, unlike them — they chattered all the time. He was tolerant of the younger children and had a serene kind of temperament not easily aroused to anger and he was sensible and mature for his age. In his Norfolk jacket, bow tie, three-quarter hose almost meeting his long shorts, he poses with his sisters, a little smile on his lips and in his eyes.

Netta, at six years the oldest girl, is round faced and serious, her light brown hair tied back in a bow. She is in her Sunday dress, made by my mother, bare legged, in short socks and black shoes. She obviously feels her responsibility to look after wee Betty and prevent her from rolling off the couch on which they sit. She was already helping Mother with the younger children and proving to be a useful assistant.

Mamie, the next in age at four years, sits on an upright chair, probably swinging her legs until the photogapher asked her to keep still! That was always difficult for her. Mamie was always full of bounce and go. She has a little smile on her face. There is an air of suppressed excitement about her, in spite of her demure appearance. She and Madeline are wearing identical dresses, my mother's work and could be taken for twins as only thirteen months separated their births.

Madeline leans against Mamie's knee and gives the photographer a straight, unsmiling look. For all their innocent expressions, those two were often involved in mischief. Mamie was usually the ringleader. Madeline could be rather dreamy at times. With her head in the clouds, she was likely to forget to turn a corner with the rest of the family and had to be rescued from time to time.

Betty, the baby, not yet walking, is firmly held in place by Netta. She is a wee fat dumpling of a child with a permanently surprised expression, not much hair, her little feet tucked under a whiter than white dress.

No great strides, in fact no strides at all, had been made to make housework easier in the decade since my mother married and set up home. She had more than a full-time job caring for her family. Even in the evenings, the house hummed with the sound of her Singer sewing machine as she made the girls' dresses. They fell asleep to its comforting sound. The machine was Mother's pride and joy with its polished wood top and its black wrought iron legs and treadle. Bought for her by my father as a prudent investment, it proved to be just that for many years.

A mountain of washing had to be done each day, except for Sundays of course, which were still sacrosanct. Although morals had slipped sadly during the war, they had not slipped far enough to allow a respectable woman to hang out a wash on a Sunday. At least not in Leith. It was a constantly running "soap opera" to keep the children cleanly dressed and my father's working shirts always ready for him. Still particular in his appearance, he went to his work and came back from it looking smarter than many a man dressed in his best clothes. Mother was fussy about her appearance too and she always made sure her crossover working pinny and dustcap were out of sight and that she and our house were clean and tidy, a good fire on, and a meal ready when my father arrived home from work.

They followed the Scottish habit of having dinner at midday, and then a high tea about 5 pm. They had no idea what "after-noon tea" meant. Some English thing they knew nothing about, they supposed Our meal at 5 o'clock consisted of a "knife and fork tea". That is, something cooked like bacon and eggs, fish and chips, macaroni and cheese, or cold meat and salad, eaten with bread and butter. Scones and jam, or biscuits followed that, all washed down with tea. We never had coffee in our house. It was the last sizeable meal of the day. We could have a cup of cocoa, or tea with bread and butter or jam if we were hungry at bedtime.

After tea, the dishes were washed and put away and then both parents set about supervising homework for the older children and preparation for bed for the younger ones. My father loved to sing to them and they would watch his face attentively as he balanced the two smallest children, one on each knee and the rest at his feet. He sang old music hall songs or songs from musical comedies. They soon learned to join in with "Sister Susie sewing shirts for soldiers", "Tell me pretty maiden" from Floradora, "Waiting at the church", "Hullo, hullo, who's your lady friend?", "The Galloping Major", "Where did you get that hat?", "Beautiful Dreamer". The list was endless. The piano on which Mother had learned her scales was at Morayfield House so there was no accompaniment. Sometimes Dad would get out his home-made fiddle and play it. His children were not impressed with his playing. In fact, they were tempted to put their hands over their ears but that would have brought a sharp reprimand for cheek! So they made faces at each other instead, making sure he could not see them.

His song and fiddle recital over, the children said their prayers. It was the traditional one which begins, "This night as I lie down to sleep", although they thought the line, "And should I die before I wake" was a bit frightening. The parents hovered to make sure no one was missed when it came to "God bless Mother, Dad, Charlie", and so on, adding grandparents, aunties and uncles too. Then they were all "tucked in" for the night. Very soon after that the parents went to bed themselves as they believed in the maxim "early to bed and early to rise, makes a man healthy, wealthy and wise".

The children were a lively bunch and they filled the little house with their chatter. Their games were the age old traditional

Scottish games which came round in their season. So peevery beds, diabolos, peeries, rounders, skipping ropes, kick-the-can and tig took their turn as if to some pre-ordained timetable. There were lots of neighbourhood children to play with so there was no shortage of players when it came to choosing sides for team games. Mother and Dad were still young and daft enough to join in and take their turn at 'ca'in' the rope for skipping. In the icy weather they had a go on the slides the children made on the long paths of the Links, mother's long skirts flapping as she went, to arrive panting and pink with exertion in my father's arms. In summer, there were picnics at Portobello beach where the children paddled blissfully in the shallows, or persuaded Dad to play a game of cricket with them. Mother looked after their discarded clothes and the picnic food. When the call came, "tea's up" they fell upon the feast of sandwiches like savages, not bothered by the gritty feel of sand if it accidentally blew onto the food. Then at the end of the day, wet swimming suits rolled up in a towel under their arm, they walked home and so to bed.

Leith Links made an ideal playground too and when the grass had been cut, the children could build a house of the new mown sweet smelling grass and pelt each other with handfuls of the stuff. Mother grumbled about all the grass being carried into the house and even into the beds but it was only a very mild grumble. They stayed out as late as they could in the long evenings. For as long as Mother would allow. They loved to run around barefoot, not from necessity but for the joy of feeling the cool grass under their toes. Mother threw down a treacle or jam "piece" to them from her window for their *al fresco* supper. A brick held the front door ajar to save her from having to go down and open it when they were ready to come in at bedtime.

Sundays, of course, were different. For a start, the children were not allowed to play in the street. None of their chums were either so it did not matter too much. They went to church and Sunday School at St John's (East) just as soon as they were old enough, wearing their best clothes. Charlie wore his Sunday suit, and the girls their Sunday dresses and coats. They wore straw hats trimmed with artificial flowers in summer and velour hats in winter. Usually they were anchored by an elastic band under the chin to prevent them flying away.

At Sunday School, in their separate classes according to age, they had to learn their Catechism, the Ten Commandments and the Lord's Prayer by heart. Each week they were given a little deckle-edged card with a spray of flowers or a nativity scene on it, on which was printed a text from the Bible to learn before the next Sunday. The teacher told them the ancient stories from the Old Testament; the nice romantic ones about David and Goliath, Joseph and his coat of many colours, Daniel in the lion's den, Jonah and the whale — never about the barbaric wars and slaughters of innocents. From the New Testament they learned the parables. They dutifully handed in their penny for the collection and sang hymns such as, "Jesus loves me", "The morning bright with rosy light" or "All things bright and beautiful". A prayer or two and they were free to go home, walking through the Links.

There were prizes to be won for attendance so there was some reward for all this devotion and the Harrises got their fair share of them. There were also the Sunday School trips and Christmas parties to be looked forward to. Often they went to more than one Sunday School when these two events were looming so that they could go to more than one trip or party, the devious little devils! The trips meant a day away from home, races to be run and won, a tuppeny pie to eat in your hand, a cake, a bun, a biscuit, all washed down with strong tea from an urn. The parties meant new party frocks of tussore, taffeta or velvet made by mother and sandwiches, sausage rolls, Christmas cake, jelly and icecream, and games to play.

On Sunday afternoons if the weather was fine, still in their Sunday best, they went for a sedate walk, feeling very grown up. No romping or loud voices were permitted to break the Sabbath. Very often their steps took them to the quietest place they knew, Seafield Cemetery. At that time there were lots of little paths they could wander along, speculating about the names they read on the stones there. If the weather was bad and they had to stay indoors that day, they played games with paper and pencil, or ludo, snakes and ladders, or tiddlywinks if someone had been lucky enough to get them for Christmas or a birthday. The girls loved to cut things out of magazines, or dress paper dolls, exchange scraps, or knit and crochet with wool left over from Mother's knitting. They sang a lot too, although they had to be careful *what* they sang on Sundays. No loud or boisterous music hall songs but suitable songs they learned at school.

As well as church and Sunday School, they were all great joiners of organisations such as choirs, Brownies, Guides, Band of Hope, and anything else that came their way.

Mother and Dad went to church regularly. Mother's church before she married was the Catholic Apostolic in Broughton Street. It was not a Catholic Church; more like High English. She went there from time to time in her early married days but gradually ceased these visits and gave the little time she had for church to St John's (East). In any case, it was the correct thing for a wife to be received into her husband's church on marriage. They were very faithful members and often attended twice on a Sunday, especially after my father became an elder. They had their own family pew in the church which they rented for a small sum each year. A little framed notice attached to the pew showed that it belonged to our family. It was certainly a bargain as we filled it to overflowing eventually and as so many of our activities stemmed from the church, we had a very long running association with it over many years.

It may seem as if those first five Harris children were a goody-goody lot and therefore insufferable prigs. This is not so. The girls all confess they were often rebellious, disobedient and cheeky. Contradicting what an adult said was a serious crime and they were often guilty. Interrupting a conversation was just as bad. It was a sore trial to them as they found it difficult to keep their mouths shut. It was so unfair. They often had to be told "children should be seen and not heard" or "empty vessels make the most sound". You had to think about that last one. If they went on a visit they had a little lecture before they left home on how they were expected to behave. After the visit, if anyone had been noisy or impolite, they were given a severe dressing down.

Netta confesses that when she was sent with a pillowcase to buy four plain loaves from the baker's, she used to strip the hot soft outside slices from the bread and eat them on the way home! They were often sent on messages to various shops and were expected to come back with the correct purchase and be able to produce the correct change. Mamie once got a good smacking from Mother when she lost 3d (less than 2 pence), a useful amount of money in those days.

On one occasion, Mother forbade them all to go to Seafield to play. They defied her and went anyway. When they got back, as a punishment for such a crime they were made to sit outside without their tea. They sat and ate paper as they were so hungry, until Mother relented and let them in for their tea. Then there was the saga of how Mother's precious sewing machine got scratched. No one owned up to that and the investigation went on for days without the culprit confessing. No one ever did, not even now!

My parents believed in corporal punishment when they thought it was justified and supported the motto "spare the rod and spoil the child", but it was left to Mother to administer it. This she did with a will and a pair of long fingered boney hands, or a swift flick of a wet dishcloth on the back of the legs. Dad never raised a hand to any of us. A severe look was as far as he went and it was enough. If one of us tried to by-pass Mother to ask for something he would say, "you'd better ask your mother" so there was no escaping her authority.

Wasting food was something my parents could not tolerate. Our plates had to be empty at the end of a meal. No finickiness was allowed and crusts had to be eaten as well as the nice bits. Fortunately, there was always a sister who liked the things another hated, so between us all we managed to leave empty plates.

Around our family at this time there were not as many relatives as before the war. Grandfather Rutherford at Morayfield still tilled his land. In his fifties now, he worked as hard as ever in the fields, helped by his labourer. His eldest grandchild, our Charlie, gives us a picture of him at that time. It seems Charlie decided he would take a school friend to the nursery to see it and assured his chum that the old man would be glad to see them. They got a shock. There stood the laird of Morayfield at the door of the house with his shotgun in his hand, his two dogs, Tinker and Nunkie at his heels! The boys turned tail and ran!

Uncle Johnny and Auntie Jean were away out of the country more often than not. When they did pay a visit to Leith to stay at Morayfield, they fairly brought a breath of excitement into the Harris family. They were like exotic cockatoos, compared with us plain Leith sparrows. They descended on us in a flurry of activity, especially Auntie Jean who "wore the breeks". Uncle

Johnny tagged along and provided the cash. They never did things by halves as they had become accustomed to nothing but the best. When they gave the Harris children a treat, no expense was spared. Once they took them to a pantomime with Tommy Lorne in it. There was a party first at Morayfield House in the spacious drawing room. How impressed the children were by the elegant stair case and beautiful carpets. Then a box at the theatre. Two taxis were hired to take the whole party.

Another time these two benefactors arranged for the family to have a week's holiday. A holiday every year away from home was the exception rather than the rule, although there was a yearly Trades Week. All that meant was that the breadwinner of the family did not work that week and did not get paid either! On this occasion the whole family went to Musselburgh in Grandfather's horse-drawn trap to stay in a house rented by Auntie Jean. The trap was beautiful, with curved wooden seats and back rests and narrow steps up to the back. One thing they remember about that holiday is that my mother had to go and buy mousetraps as the house was overrun with mice!

There were picnics too and as Uncle Johnny had a taste for big, flashy cars, the Harris family felt like millionaires for a short time as they swept past their less fortunate chums as to the manner born. No doubt about it, Auntie Jean and Uncle Johnny added spice to the lives of the family with their unfailing generosity. They never made us feel like poor relations either. When they went off again on their travels, a certain excitement disappeared with them.

Our Auntie Mary only came back to Morayfield occasionally. Romance had entered her life and she married a soldier she met while nursing the wounded. He had been gassed in the war. They lived in Glasgow for a while but eventually, as Harry was an Englishman, they moved with their son to England. She visited us from time to time, still cheerful and good natured. In looks she was very like my mother, only a little plumper.

Tom, my father's brother had trained as a jeweller. He emigrated to America after the war. He hoped he would find more opportunities there than in Leith. He had prepared a box of jewellery as a basis for a business in America and set off with high hopes. On his arrival at Customs, his precious box was confiscated, leaving him with no assets and no return ticket. He survived that calamity somehow and prospered in spite of it. He married in America and named one of his daughters Madeline, after his mother. Contact with Tom was rather spasmodic over the years, especially after his mother died and finally broke down completely after the Second World War.

Will, the other brother, invalided out of the army after the war, still lived in Leith with his wife and two daughters. We saw them from time to time. Will's war service left his health impaired as his lungs had been affected by mustard gas. He found it hard to find suitable work as a result, but he managed to survive and support his wife and family with the help of an Army pension.

The youngest of that family, Annie, was now twenty-nine years old, still unmarried. On the shelf; an old maid; an unclaimed treasure. She still lived with her mother, Granny Brown and Henderson Brown, with their two children.

The neighbours had hardly changed at all since before the war, and the same closeknit community was clustered happily next to the cemetery gates. They were all hard working people, labourers and tradesmen bringing up their families to a strict code of conduct instilled in them by their own upbringing.

My mother and father were the same kind of people. They took their purpose in life seriously and allowed nothing to distract them from it. They now had four children at school and the youngest was about to start school next year. To keep them fed and healthy was their main aim and they were doing very well, so far.

CHAPTER 8

The three kids

How, in March 1919, my mother reacted to the knowledge that she was pregnant again is not recorded. She never in later years told any of us. According to her upbringing, it was not a subject for conversation anyway. Even when we were all grown up and having babies of our own, we had no woman-to-woman talks on the subject of pregnancy and childbirth.

Nowadays, she would be termed a "geriatric" mother as she was 33 years old. With Betty soon to start school, she had probably envisaged an easier way of life for herself and now here she was back in the old "hippen" routine. However, with her usual calm acceptance of the inevitable, she began to make barracots and nightgowns and to knit the pilches, vests, matinee jackets and shawls so essential for a baby's layette. Her precious sewing machine proved its worth now. I should explain that a barracot was a long open-sided garment made of fine flannel, with ties at the sides meant to make nappy changing easy. A pilch was a pair of knitted knickers which went over the nappy and rubber pants. All of these garments are superseded now by the ubiquitous babygro.

My father, once he got used to the idea, dug out the old pram which needed renovation. It had been used to collect coal during the war and was definitely the worse for wear. He also made a new crib, as the old one had been passed on to someone else. So that summer was spent in preparation but that autumn something happened which the first five children never forgot. Over the years it provided a subject for laughter and reminiscence although at the time it was no laughing matter.

In October, a week or two before the new baby was due to arrive, an epidemic of scarlet fever broke out in Leith. There was hardly a family which did not have some members laid low with the disease. The ambulance had a busy time carting off the sick children. In our family, first Mamie, then Betty, drooped, and fell ill. My mother, heavily pregnant and due to give birth at any time, must have been worried sick as it was a serious disease then. What a time for a new baby to arrive! When our doctor was called in and diagnosed the dreaded fever, he arranged for Mamie and Betty to be taken to the City Hospital. Then he caught sight of Madeline playing quietly on the floor nearby. "She might as well go too," he said. So the three of them were loaded into the ambulance. Betty put up some resistance. "I want to see ma Mammy's face," she yelled as she was driven away.

At the hospital chaos reigned. The harassed nurses did their best to cope. The wards were so crowded that beds had to be shared. Our Betty, as vocal as ever, objected to sharing a bed with another little girl as she "didn't want to sleep wi' a laddie". They had all had their hair cropped short so they all looked like laddies, including Betty. Well, she was only four years old. It must have been quite a shock for all those children yanked from their homes and not allowed to have contact with visitors, although they could see and wave to people through a glass partition. At first they were too unwell to care. It must have been more difficult to control them when they began to recover.

Back at Pirniefield, my poor mother, with three of her children in hospital and her sixth child about to be born, could not have been in a very tranquil state to face the hard work of the labour in front of her. The very day she gave birth to her second son, Netta was carted off to hospital leaving her with Charlie and the new baby. Netta remembers kissing her new brother before she went off in the ambulance. What a risk for a day old baby to be subjected to!

Every evening when the *Edinburgh Evening News* arrived, my mother scanned the hospital bulletin which was published each night, to see how her children were progressing. Each patient was allotted a number which would be included in various categories such as, "Dangerously ill, friends requested to come out". Fortunately, her family never appeared in that list. "Seriously ill; no immediate danger", "Improving slowly", "Not quite so well, no cause for anxiety" were little better news. But the best news of all was, "It may be concluded that all patients whose numbers are not referred to in this bulletin are making satisfactory progress".

Probably when Mother knew that the girls were on the mend, she savoured the unaccustomed peace and quiet which allowed her to recover from the birth and enjoy her new baby.

Although she had been last to go into hospital, Netta was first to come home. Then it was Mamie's turn, and then Betty.

The matron in charge of the ward our Betty was in was absolutely affronted when she announced loudly, "my mother's brasses are cleaner than yours!" They probably were but matron took strong exception and Betty was made to clean all the brasses in the ward for the rest of her stay. She was the one who had changed most in hospital and came out like a force-fed little goose. Cheekier than ever too. My father collected her at the hospital and took her home. Mother was standing at the corner of Pirniefield Place with the new baby in her arms when they arrived. She looked at Betty, then at Dad, and said, "That's not our Betty." Dad, the craven coward, said "That's the bairn they gave me," thereby putting the blame squarely on the hospital authorities. They agreed that they would wait until she was put to bed that night, and if she passed their pre-arranged test, it was definitely Betty. Sure enough, after she was tucked up in bed she shouted "I want a crust!" The parents looked at one another laughing and said simultaneously, "That's Betty alright." She had passed the test. It makes you wonder what they would have done if she had not!

Poor Madeline who had been rounded up so reluctantly with the others was last to go home. She had been "more sinned against than sinning". If she had been left at home she might not have had the fever at all.

Amidst all this excitement and coming and going, the birth of the baby passed practically unnoticed. When they got round to it he was christened James, after his grandfather. Of course, Dad was delighted to have another son among all these girls. Mother must have had to work very hard to keep up with all the work she had to do in the small flat. It was bursting at the seams now. The older children had to learn very fast to help with the baby. What was really desperately needed was a larger house but larger houses cost more in rent. Their budget was tight enough as it was and there was no hope of that for a while yet.

In the year of Jim's birth, it became evident that once more Leith was under the threat of losing its identity if it was to be absorbed by the City of Edinburgh. This had been a threat many times in the past but perhaps the ordinary Leith citizen was a bit slow to realise what had almost become inevitable. Who could blame them? After all, they had elected Town Councillors to deal with that kind of business and they were expected to do the job properly. The Council however, failed to lodge its objection to the takeover promptly enough. Eventually in January 1920, it was decided to take a plebiscite. As it had been delayed so long, the plebiscite had to be organised very quickly before the deadline for objections was past. In spite of the fact that the result of the plebiscite showed that there was an overwhelming vote against amalgamation, the takeover went through just the same. There were angry protest marches and demonstrations but nothing could change it now.

Our parents spoke of this disaster in later years, shaking their heads in regret as they did so. To us going to school and church, seeing Leith as it then was, a bustling, living, vibrant town, we still had a fierce loyalty to the place in the twenties and thirties. Any Leither will tell you that that loyalty is still alive today just as it was among citizens past. We all thought sunny Leith was a great place to live and grow up in. And we still do.

Soon another member of the family was about to get married and was preparing to shed the dust of Leith from her feet, our Auntie Annie, she who had been taught by my father to play bools as a baby. She was over thirty now and although there were no very young marriages in our family, at her age, it was a surprise, she was a bit "over the hill" to be thought of as still of marriageable age, or so it had been assumed. However, she met and fell in love with an officer in the Royal Navy serving on HMS *The Royal Oak*. Family memories do not give us any information about how they met or how long a courtship they had.

In June 1921 they had a traditional white wedding. Annie wore the long, shapeless, waistless dress fashionable in the twenties, a long veil with her headdress well down over her brows, white shoes and stockings.

The reception was a swell affair at the Assembly Rooms in Leith and the whole of the Harris family was there. In fact, you could say that even I went to that wedding as my mother, whose deplorable contraceptive methods, if any, had let her down yet again, was four months pregnant with me! The girls were all in their Sunday dresses and on their best behaviour. They had had the usual little homily from my mother on how to behave, which was routine on occasions like this. Our Jim, not yet two years old, disgraced himself even before we got to the wedding. He was sent outside to wait until the the rest of the family was ready and managed to get tar on his new tussore suit!

Auntie Jean and Uncle Johnny provided their large limousine to take us to the wedding and it was a memorable event by all accounts. Auntie Annie, bless her heart, sang a most affecting song "Take me back to bonnie Scotland" and then went off with her handsome husband to settle in England. She visited us occasionally in later years — I can recall her with dangly earrings swinging from her ears. By then she had acquired a soft English accent and looked curiously like my father.

I expect by the time I was born on 24th November 1921, the others were completely blasé about the constant additions to their numbers. They had no clue from whence they came either. No one told them the facts of life. When Mother went into labour, the older ones were sent to the Laurie picture house, best seats 3d, bench seats 1d. The younger ones were bundled off to neighbours. The film they saw was called "The Yellow Mire". It must have been an early horror film. It scared the wits out of them so that afterwards they always associated it with my birth! It hardly sounds a suitable choice for children but I expect my mother had no time to think about that when her labour began. My father was at work, the best place for him. Fathers were not welcome at the bedside of expectant mothers. Granny Brown, who had probably attended all her previous confinements, saw my mother successfully through this one.

When the children returned, everything was clean and tidy and there was Mother lying in the bed in the recess with her new little bundle. They must have viewed it with some apprehension. They knew from past experience that, wherever it came from, it meant wheeling a pram, lots of nappies flapping on the clothes line or steaming damply before the fire, crowded sleeping arrangements, and a mother too busy to play with them. It was fortunate that none of the children was sickly at birth and very quickly took a good grip on life as, according to modern experts, at least one or two of them should have fallen by the wayside, victims of the many illnesses lying in wait for them.

My father's part in the process of my birth was to register it with the local registrar. This he did by the skin of his teeth, on the very last day of the twenty-one days allowed. He was by this time what you might call a very "laid back" dad!

The following February, I was baptised at St John's and given the name Agnes, after my mother. Later on in my life I always hated giving my full name which revealed the awful truth that my first name was Agnes. I often reproached my mother about it. Luckily, the family and everyone else always called me "Nancy". All of us were called after someone in the older generation. All our names were fairly plain but we knew Euphemias, Alexandras and Dorothys, usually shortened to Phemie, Lexie and Dot. In Mother's generation there were plenty of Teenies, Lizzies and Aggies. Perhaps they will come back into fashion in the future .

When I was only six months old, Grandfather Rutherford fell ill and took to his bed at Morayfield House. He was the kind of man who would not give in to illness, or even recognise its presence. He more than likely continued with his work knowing he was unwell, but trying to fight it off. The result was that by the time his wife managed to persuade him to go to bed, it was too late. His illness became pneumonia and he died in May 1922 at the age of 59 years.

It was a sad time for the family. Uncle Johnny came back to Leith with Auntie Jean to attend the funeral and to deal with the legal matters involved. The funeral was celebrated with due pomp and ceremony. There was a service in the drawing room at Morayfield House and an impressive cortège to Seafield Cemetery. There he was laid to rest beside his first wife, Janet and their first child who had lived for such a short time so long ago.

The tenancy of Morayfield was continued for a few months until Martinmas in November while Uncle Johnny wound up the estate. The furniture at Morayfield House was either sold or passed to members of the family. Mother took possession of her piano and one or two other pieces. My mother's share in the estate was £1,000, which was a sizeable sum then.

My mother at that time must have once again decided that her family was complete as she arranged to have a photograph of the family taken with Granny Brown. Charlie is in his first suit of long trousers and Mamie, Betty, Netta and Madeline look as if butter would not melt in their mouths. Jim is leaning against Granny with his arm through hers, probably in the very tussore suit he wore at Auntie Annie's wedding. I am sitting on Granny's knee. As usual, my mother was wrong and by the end of that year she knew she was pregnant again.

Early in 1923, my parents began to make plans which would change the life of the family and bring us more prosperity. With the money left to my mother, it was decided that my father should look for premises and set up his own business. This was something he had long hoped for. He rented a piece of ground from the Roperie Company in James Lane, Leith, and then with his own hands, he set about building his workshop on the site. He bought second-hand wood, doors, windows, anything which could be useful to him. He must have worked long hours to complete it. After that he had to buy wood and other supplies to stock it. Then the various sawing machinery, tools and electricity had to be installed. It was a happy time for him and he already had the promise of work whenever his workshop was ready. What a day that must have been when he was able to put up his sign announcing to all that "C.J. Harris, Joiner and Shopfitter" was open for business. There was no champagne celebration, just my father whistling as he worked in his own workshop with the tools and materials he loved.

In March that year, Henderson Brown died and Granny Brown was once more a widow. Her first family were all married. Her second family were grown up and the hardships of the past were behind her. After a while she moved round into Seafield Avenue where she spent the rest of her days.

My mother gave birth to Jean, my wee sister, in August. Very soon, under the influence of American slang which had begun to invade the country by means of the cinema, Jim, Jean and I came to be known as "the three kids". Jean was only one year and nine months younger than I, so my mother now had three bairns under five, as well as all the older ones. The girls had to help quite a lot in looking after the three kids, something they did not neglect to mention to us in later years! I was Netta's special responsibility, so that Mother could attend to the demands of the new baby. How strange it is to think that in the year Jean was born, my brother Charlie left school at the age of fourteen to join my father as his apprentice, and the year after that, Netta left school to become my father's clerkess.

Now that my father's business was set up, my parents began to look for a larger house to accommodate our large family. They chose one in the terraces off Lochend Road which they bought for £350. It was paid for with what remained of Grandfather's legacy. They are known as colony houses now, and I believe much sought after. They were built in 1861. The name of each terrace has a woodland flavour such as, 'Ashville', 'Oakville' and 'Thornville'. Ours was 'Woodbine'. It was built in such a way that no horse or motor traffic could get along it. Any traffic other than foot traffic had to stop at the end of the terrace. Consequently, it was an ideal safe area for children. Probably my parents had this in mind when they chose it.

The flitting took place in September 1924 when I was almost three years old. It was a fine dry day and everything was piled onto a horse-drawn cart and secured with ropes. Then the procession set off, the older children walking beside the horse.

Mother was left behind at Pirniefield to make sure everything was left clean and tidy for the next tenant of the top flat which had seen so many births, and where she had first set up home as a married woman. When she was ready, she piled Jean and me into the go-car and with Jim half running at her side to keep up with her long strides, she followed the procession along Blackie Road to Restalrig Road, through Restalrig Terrace to Lochend Road and the terraces.

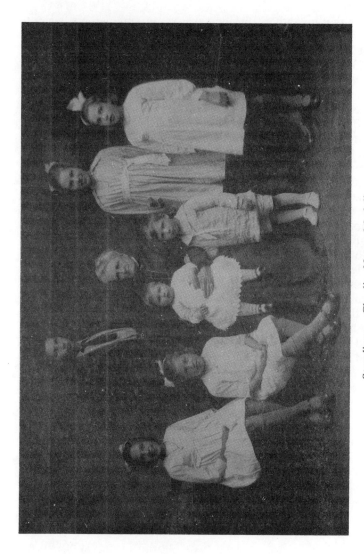

Standing — Charlie, Netta, Madeline
Seated — Mamie, Betty, Nancy, Granny Brown, Jim, 1922

CHAPTER 9

Pastures new

Our new home in Woodbine Terrace was bigger than the flat at Pirniefield. There was a flight of stairs shared with our next door neighbour, then a stout wooden main door and an inner glass door. On that floor when we moved in, there was a kitchen/living room with a sink at the window, a small room adjoining that, a lavatory, a bedroom and a parlour. At first Jean, only a baby then, slept in a crib in the small room next to the kitchen. Dad fixed a mirror on the wall in such a way that we could see her and check on her without disturbing her. Charlie, the lucky lad, slept in the small bedroom upstairs in solitary splendour. The rest of us, including Jim who was only five years old, occupied the large bedroom. There was plenty of room for the two double and two single beds which were soon installed and occupied. There was a fireplace and an ornamental overmantel with a large mirror in the room. The fire was only lit on very special occasions, in later years if Jean and I were dressing for a party. It did nothing to heat the room, but it did a lot for our morale as we shivered into our party frocks. It made the occasion just a little bit special.

My parents occupied the bedroom downstairs. Even when we were all grown up, Dad always propped open the door with one of his slippers when he went to bed so that he could hear us if we called out in the night and needed anything.

As there was no hot water and no bath it might look as if, apart from more space, we had gained nothing by our move. Soon, however, my father set about making improvements. He built in a Chatinette grate in the kitchen, the very latest household appliance, with two ovens, a tiled surround, a copper canopy and most important of all, a back boiler to give hot water. What a change from the old black range which had ruled my mother's life at Pirniefield. This grate still needed to be stoked with coal but it was much more efficient, clean and more compact than the range. Although the fire was not meant to be used for cooking, except for the ovens, thrift had been so much instilled into my mother that if there was a good fire on, she would heat a kettle on it rather than waste money heating it on the new Main gas cooker. The saving must have been infinitesimal.

When Jean was old enough to be promoted to the big bedroom upstairs, my father divided the little room she had occupied to form a scullery entered from the kitchen and a bathroom entered from the lobby. Then he installed a tub and sink in the scullery and as much shelving as he could fit in. Later on he installed electricity. What a wonder that was for the children. They were often in trouble for playing with the light on the stairs as, of course, you could switch it on at the bottom of the stairs and off at the top. It was nothing short of a miracle to them. Mother never quite got used to the magic of electricity either, or to the idea that light bulbs did not use much of the stuff. We were often in trouble for leaving a light on in an empty room. What she would say now that many of us leave several lights on in an empty house, let alone one room as a safety measure, one cringes to think!

All these alterations took place over a period of years but, of course, with my mother in mind as ever, the hot water and the bath came first. I can imagine my Mother's joy at being able to have hot water on tap for her weekly wash and to have a bath so readily available. Of course, it was still quite a hefty job to keep up with washing clothes for such a large family. Mother had an Acme wringer now, a great step forward but she still had to rub the clothes on a ridged scrubbing board. Then she had to carry them down the stairs in a wicker basket to the small garden with its rectangle of grass and neat flower beds. Like the first five children, we hated washing days. When we arrived for our midday dinner from school to the scene of action, we grabbed our meal and went straight out again, overcome by the mixed scents of bleach, washing soap and mince and tatties which met us at the door.

Our kitchen was the hub and centre of the life of our home. It had best quality linoleum on the floor, a fireside rug, the kitchen table, two small armchairs, one or two upright chairs, a wooden stool or two and the kitchen dresser. We relaxed, played, talked, sang, argued, fought, read books, did our homework often with all Hell let loose around us, in that room. We had no movable electric fires in any of the other rooms and the parlour with its gas fire was out of bounds. There was always a coal fire in the kitchen, so that was where we all congregated for whatever reason. How we all fitted into it when we were all at home is a mystery, but we managed. After all, we had lived in even more cramped conditions so we were experts. The house in Woodbine seemed enormous after Pirniefield.

Our parlour was set aside for special occasions. There was carpeting on the floor, two comfortable upholstered and anti-macassared armchairs and a matching bed-settee, the piano, and the gramophone. This special room was a sign of our improved status and parlours like ours were to be found all over Leith and Edinburgh. They are there still, although more likely to be called the front room, lounge, sitting room, or drawing room. It is almost as though your prosperity could be measured by the number of unused rooms you had in your house. When I met the boy who became my husband, I was invited by his parents to their home for a meal. I was astounded to find that they had three rooms kept for best. A best bedroom, a drawing room, and a dining room. Just fancy a whole room set aside to eat in! They had a large kitchen and a large scullery and that was where all the action was. In fact, during the Second World War when air raid warnings were frequent, they even slept in the kitchen, leaving three upstairs bedrooms unused, as well as the two rooms downstairs.

To come back to our parlour, although it was meant for visitors, we were allowed to practice on the piano when we were taking lessons and to play the gramophone, provided we left everything tidy. The furnishings, as in the rest of our house, remained the same all our time there. Things were built to last. There was no pressure to keep up with "the Joneses". My parents had their own standards and envied no one.

My own memories of my earliest days at Woodbine are few but I do remember the occasion when the family all went to a pantomime. I had to be left behind because I had measles. I yelled blue murder. I pity whoever was left in charge of me that night. They must have had a rough time of it.

The only other memories of those early days are of my father taking me on one knee and Jean on the other and singing especially for me:-

"Nancy Nancy I hope that you will be true.
Every night and every day I always dream
of you.
Now I'm sailing to the west,
Back to the lassie I lo'e the best.
Nancy you're my fancy and my real true blue."

I was bewitched to have a song with my own name in it. But Jean, who listened with barely concealed impatience to this paean, would start wriggling and say loudly and imperiously JEAN, JEAN, whereupon Dad would turn to her and sing the song with her name in it, which went:-

"Jean, Jean, ma bonnie bonnie Jean,
Come to ma airms once again.
For although your feet are flat,
you're nane the waur o' that,
You're my bonnie blue eyed Scots lassie, Jean."

This satisfied Jean and allowed Dad to go on to some of the other songs in his vast repertoire. We were as entranced as our older sisters had been by his performance. The fiddle must have been laid aside by this time, as I have no memory of it.

Our new surroundings were very different from Pirniefield. We could play in the small garden, or in the traffic-free terrace. Leith Links and Portobello, although farther away, were not too far for our young legs to go. On one side we had no neighbours at all as our house was the last one in the row and the grounds of St Anthony's School adjoined us. Had we but known it, our Jim was destined to teach there in later years. We soon came to know our neighbours. They were working people, tradesmen of various kinds, office workers, bank clerks, shop assistants, a policeman or two, most of them church goers and pillars of the community. However, in those days it was not the done thing for neighbours to be in and out of each other's houses, as is sometimes the case now. They were as ignorant about coffee mornings as they were about afternoon tea. Of course, my mother with her large family and no help in the house would have found it difficult to spare time for such diversions.

We soon found friends of our own age. Some of the friends Jim made then are still his friends today. He went into the Second World War with them and out the other side. Jean and I found many friends too and there was always a big crowd of us to play rounders or kick-the-can.

Since our move to another area, our shopping habits had to change too. We bought most of our groceries from "the Store" just up Lochend Road, not far from us. They had a "fleshing" department and a bakery which were well patronised by us. If we were sent up to the butcher for mince, Mother said we were to ask for "a pound of lean round steak, please", then when the butcher had cut it, we were to say "mince it please". This was because the ready minced stuff in the window had more fat in it, or so Mother thought. The butcher always glowered at us as if we had played a trick on him. Of course we had!

We always bought our vegetables and fruit from Mr Pearce who came round the terraces with his horse and cart, ringing his handbell. The housewives congregated round his mobile shop taking the opportunity to have a blether, as well as to buy his fresh vegetables. In summer, another caller was the icecream man on his bicycle. It was specially adapted to carry his container of icecream with the slogan "Stop me and buy one" on the side. The sound of his whistle galvanized us into action to beg a penny for a slider or a cone. What bliss on a hot summer day, although if you ate it too fast you got a cracking headache warning you to slow up.

There was a small shop just at the entrance to the terraces which stocked a wide variety of goods as well as sweets. It was into that shop's till that most of our Saturday pennies went and it was to that shop we had to run if Mother found she was short of some essential ingredient for the stew.

Down Lochend Road, just before you came to Primrose Street, which in those days was a pretty run down place, there was a lovely high class grocer shop called Kennedy's. It was there we went to buy dried fruit for a special cake, or demerara or soft brown sugar. It was like Aladdin's cave to us as we looked round the shelves, with our eyes popping at the luxury goods they stocked. Exotic jars of ginger stood next to glass jars full of whole or ground almonds. Maraschino cherries, angelica, vanilla and cinnamon sticks. There was a range of small labelled drawers with intriguing contents. We could never quite read the labels, but even if we had been able to, it probably would have meant nothing to us.

The shop assistants, in spotless white coats, presided over their long counter, cutting into enormous cheddar cheeses with a wire cutter, or taking pounds of butter from a big barrel to bash it into shape with two wooden paddles. Any slack time they had they spent weighing out pounds of granulated, caster or icing sugar, or tea. Their expert fingers filled the pale brown paper bags and closed them neatly so that they looked as if a machine had made them. Very clever, we thought. Hardly anything was pre-packed in those days and you could buy as small a quantity as you wished without the assistants looking down their noses at you. There was a also a bank of biscuit tins with glass tops so you could see the biscuits. There was an infinite variety to choose from. The assistants weighed out your choice of biscuits, or mixed them for you. There might even be the chance of buying broken biscuits at a reduced price. We were not too proud to take advantage of that.

On the floor, there were great sacks of flour of all kinds, rice, sago, tapioca, lentils, split peas, barley, haricot beans, oatmeal. Your fingers itched to dig into them. At the end of the counter stood a big bacon slicing machine. You chose your bacon and specified the thickness you wanted, and the assistant turned the machine handle to slice it for you.

A few doors from Kennedy's there was a paper shop called Young's run by the two Misses Jarvis, who incidentally lived across the terrace from us. Basically a newsagents shop, they sold a variety of other interesting things. Pens, inks, stationery, glue, erasers, rulers, notebooks, account books for all purposes, games like ludo, snakes and ladders, tiddlywinks, playing cards, comics and children's books. Jean and I always bought our "Fairyland Tales" and our "scraps" there. In fact, if you were looking for some obscure item, you went to Young's first before looking farther afield and nine times out of ten they produced it from their wee back shop in no time. At Christmas time they had a row of dolls and calendars hanging up over the counter so that neither parents nor children had to look very far for what Santa Claus was expected to bring.

These two spinster ladies always had a smile for their customers. I never saw them angry or impatient. Many a time my father said "that shop must be a wee goldmine". If it was, these two ladies deserved it. Of medium height with grey hair, eyes twinkling behind their pince-nez specs, they instinctively knew how to treat each customer and their shop was always busy.

They also ran a penny-a-week library. I should think the Harris family just about read all the novels in it. Although we patronised McDonald Road Library, we often borrowed from Young's as it was on our way home from work.

In that area too there was a wee sweetie shop. I think it was simply the front room of a house adapted for the purpose. We used to buy fizzy drinks like 'Vimto' and 'Tizer' there. They displayed some of the goods in little saucers. There were tiger nuts, liquorice root, aniseed balls, locust beans, shredded coconut with a chocolate powder coating, peanuts in their shells, all laid out for us to choose from. On the shelves were jars containing such exotic delights as, soor plooms, acid drops, bullseyes, jelly beans, rosy lips, conversation lozenges, dolly mixtures, liquorice allsorts, an amazing variety for such a tiny shop. It was well patronised by some of the school children on the way to and from school. Not by the Harrises though. We never had any money to spend during the school week as we had spent our Saturday pennies by Monday. Some of the kids who had money for sweets obviously had none left for soap and water or darning wool!

There was a shoemender in that area as well but we seldom needed his services, at least not until we left school and began buying "fashion" shoes which Dad would have nothing to do with. He did all our shoe repairs up to that time. He soaked the thick leather in the scullery sink and cut it to shape with a sharp knife. Then with a shoemaker's last across his knees, which he called his "devil's foot", he nailed the soles on. He made a good job of them too. Sometimes he hammered segs into the heels to prevent them wearing too quickly.

At the foot of Lochend Road there was a hairdresser who also got very little business from us. While Jean and I were at school, Dad cut our hair. He cut it neatly to ear lobe length with a straight fringe. If we wanted to grow our fringes to have a side parting with a clasp to hold the hair in place, he only cut the bottom.

In Duke Street, the first shop on the corner with Easter Road was Spence the Chemist. Farther along there was Jimmy Howe's, Gents' Outfitters where my father and many other men in Leith bought their Sunday suits, shirts and ties. Then there was a confectioner's. It was definitely not a wee sweetie shop. As well as high quality icecream, they sold the more expensive range of sweets and chocolates. They had in their window Callard and Bowser's Butterscotch, Basset's Liquorice Allsorts, Edinburgh Rock, Berwick Cockles, sugared almonds, home-made tablet and treacle toffee, Fry's Chocolate Cream, Cadbury's Plain and Milk Chocolate in big bars, Terry's Bitter Chocolate, Parisian Creams, Mint Imperials, Curiously Strong Mints, exotic boxes of chocolates, and usually bang in the middle of the window, a great tray of thick milk chocolate studded all over with enormous Brazil nuts. How I longed for that Brazil nut chocolate but it was too expensive. Our preferences in those days were not very discriminating and the cheaper the better.

We delighted in liquorice straps, nailrod, sugarollie, sherbet dabs, snowballs, macaroon bars, puff candy, Highland toffee, charm tatties, Polisman's Gundy, chocolate drops, and anything else guaranteed to rot our teeth. You can still find some of them in Edinburgh and Leith, if you know where to look. At Christmas time of course, we loved to discover in the toe of our Christmas stocking, a pink or white sugar mouse or pig, or a little net bag of chocolate money, each "coin" wrapped in its own silver or gold paper. Yes, there were sweets for all tastes. In winter we could buy Winter Mixture, cough drops, Victory V Lozenges, Zubes, Liquorice Linseed and Chlorodyne lozenges known as L.L. and C. Lozenges, all designed to warm you up. A farthing or a ha'penny bought quite a lot of sweet pleasure depending on whether you were a "sooker" or a "cruncher". I am a "cruncher"!

In Duke Street there was also a chip shop which was much patronised by my sisters and myself. People who worked in shops or offices in Edinburgh and got the tram or train to the Foot of the Walk, were often attracted by the intoxicating smell from that shop. If it was pay day, they bought a fish or pie supper to take home and eat for their tea. If funds were low, it was tuppence-worth of peas and vinegar. Nothing tasted quite so good as those suppers. Wrapped in newspaper and clutched to your bosom, you could feel the heat and smell them all the way home. If you were fussy, you decanted them on to a plate. If not, you ate straight out of the paper!

In my teens there was a café in Duke Street which was popular with us. We would sit with a cup of coffee and talk by the hour about this and that, setting the world to rights. In fact, a lot of hot air. As with all generations, we came to the conclusion that our parents had made a real hash of running the world and that we could do better. The owners of that café must have been very understanding as they never asked us to leave, even although we were occupying seats and not spending much. It was warm and comfortable there on a winter's night and we were very regular customers.

Across the street there was another place associated with enjoyment. Smith's Rooms, scene of many a social function and wedding reception of Leith folk. I recall an occasion there when I wore my first long party dress. It was made of pink crêpe and gold lamé, which must have been in fashion then. My sister Madeline made it for me and I thought I looked very chic. They still had dances like the Polka, the Paul Jones and the Valeta on the programmes then, as well as The Dashing White Sergeant and Eightsomes. I enjoyed them all.

Woolworths at the Foot of the Walk held a great attraction for us. What a variety of goods they offered. Their claim that everything was 3d or 6d must have been difficult to fulfill sometimes but they managed it. For example, a teapot might cost 6d and its lid 3d. My mother always bought her everyday china there and as each item was separately priced, it was easy to replace our frequent breakages.

Although there were plenty of assistants in Woolworths to help you, no one minded if you wanted to browse and then not buy anything at all. What a smashing place it was if you were caught in a shower. You could tour the counters until the rain stopped. It was one of the few shops you could go into without a penny in your pocket without feeling embarrassed.

There was a whole counter, almost the length of the shop, devoted to jewellery of all kinds, brooches, wedding and engagement rings, earrings, bracelets, necklaces, tie pins, and hat pins. Another was loaded with every possible variety of handkerchiefs you could imagine, vast areas of buttons, buckles and belts, ready-made jabots, collars and cuffs, as well as trimmings by the yard in lace and cotton. And the sweets, a vast selection to make your mouth water. They sold spectacles too. There was nothing scientific about it. You just tried on pair after pair until you found one to suit you. If you could read the test card, you bought them. My parents did not approve of this unscientific way of buying glasses, so we always went to a reputable optician for ours.

On the corner of Duke Street and Leith Walk was the Central Station where my sisters got the train each morning which took them up to Waverley Station and to the shops in which they worked. Very quick it was too. They bought a weekly Zone Ticket which saved them buying a ticket each time they travelled. Saving that little bit of time was very important to them, as they usually caught the train by the skin of their teeth. They had their morning routine timed to the last second, in order to stay in bed as long as possible. It was a mad rush in our house every morning until they all flew out of the door, leaving Mother to help us get ready for school in a more leisurely way.

In Leith Walk itself, Jeffrey's had their shop which sold curtain materials, table and bed linen. Across the Walk stood the Alhambra Picture House which Mother and Dad patronised before the Capital Cinema was built in Manderston Street. My father had a personal interest in the Alhambra as he had helped to build it when he was younger.

On that side too stood McCartney's the Butchers. We thought their sausages were the best to be had in Leith and bought a regular supply every week. Round in Great Junction Street, Egner's the Butchers also received regular visits from us. No Sunday morning breakfast was complete without their black pudding. Further along there was Smith's the Grocers, a shop rather like Kennedy's in Lochend Road, but larger and busier. The counter assistants were very quick and, of course, we got personal attention.

The big "Store" emporium, in other words Leith Provident Co-operative Wholesale Society, was situated at the far end of Great Junction Street and it was there that we bought most of our school uniforms, underwear, dresses, skirts, hats and footwear. You had a shop assistant all to yourself for a while and if you chose something to try on, she escorted you to a fitting room and then left you, coming back in a short time to see how you were getting on and to give you her opinion. Then she asked if there was anything else you would like to try and she would go off to get you a different size or colour. She might have ideas of her own about what might suit you. There was great skill in this as the shop assistant had to size up each customer and assess at a glance her size, her character and her financial status. They made very few mistakes. I imagine that not many customers came back to exchange things. If the customer needed the hem lifted or lengthened, the assistant sent for a dressmaker from their workroom. She pinned up the alteration which was free of charge and was able to say when it would be ready for collection. Usually it took a day or two. You could also take things "on approbation". That meant you could try things on in your own home. You returned them within three days and paid for the garment of your choice, or returned them all rejected.

As in their food shops, you gave the assistant your share number so that the amount of your purchase was added to your account and qualified for the "store divvy".

We came to know these shops intimately because we all at various times did Mother's shopping on a Saturday morning.

Of course, there were some deliveries and services which were brought to our door. There was the postie and the milkman, the Kleen-e-ze man with his suitcase of brushes, the man from the Prudential who came to collect the insurance money. Our parents had "Penny a week" insurance for each of us, taken out when we were born. This was not so that we would have a nice lump sum to play with in the future. No, it was to cover our funeral expenses. It sounds pessimistic but they considered it sensible to take such precautions.

Another casual caller was the Minister. Mother always made a cup of tea for him. It was all part of the ritual. On one occasion when Mother recognised his silhouette at the door, she turned to us and said, "It's the Minister, get the gun!" It may seem a pretty drastic way of dealing with the situation. He was quite a nice man, always welcome in our house. However, we all knew what she meant and hurried to light the gas with the flint gadget she called "the gun" to heat a kettle of water for tea! We often teased her about that!

The "tablet" woman was a regular caller. She came round the doors selling her homemade tablet. Small and thin, shabbily but cleanly dressed, we always asked her what kind she had. We knew very well what she had but wanted to hear her say in her genteel voice, "I've got white, pink, and vanilla, and coconut". We always bought some!

The coalman paid regular visits, shouldering his bags of coal the length of our terrace and tipping the contents into the cellar under our outside stair.

About twice a year the sweep came at Mother's invitation. He arrived at 7 am black as the lum he was to sweep, calling, "hoo hoo hoo" up the chimney and listening for an answering call from his mate to identify the correct lum. His visit always prompted a flurry of extra cleaning to get rid of the light dusting of soot he left behind him. The house was in turmoil for days. We knew that if the lum was not swept regularly it could catch fire and there would be trouble with the authorities. It never happened to us but nothing pleased us more than to hear the cry, "there's a lum up". We would watch the sparks and smoke shooting out of some hapless housewife's lum until it was brought under control. It was even better if the fire engines had to be called out.

We had a busy doorbell as our chums used to ring it to ask if we were coming out to play. A year or two after we moved in, it was boyfriends calling for the older girls who stood shyly at the door asking for one of them. With so many females, it was a standing family joke that when our doorbell rang someone would be sure to call out, "If it's a man, lock 'im in". We never tired of the joke.

Although the twenties and thirties are considered to have been a time of unemployment and depression, the Harris family were very fortunate in that they were neither unemployed nor depressed. In retrospect, most of our neighbours seemed to be just as lucky. We were not all that well off either but we always had enough food to eat, and enough clothes to wear, but no fancy luxuries. During these years my father's business prospered. He had to work long hours but when the older ones began to leave school and go out to work the burden on him became lighter year by year. When we were all working it was a family joke that every Friday evening Mother held out her "daidlie" or tea apron, for each of us to put his or her wage packet into! We had to learn to pay our way and she administered a sensible system accepted by all of us. It was not too rigid, so that if we wanted to buy a big item of clothing like a coat, she lent us the money and we paid it back to her in instalments. It worked very well.

Mother and Dad never bought things "on tick" and the only things resembling credit were the Store Book and the Mutuality Club, both run by the Co-op. Into the first Mother paid a Pound or two a week, to cover her groceries and into the second, a shilling or so to cover clothes purchases which were less frequent. We were never in debt. Our house was in my mother's name with no mortgage. The workshop and its machinery and stock belonged to Dad. Their household bills were paid promptly and in cash. I never heard them lamenting about the local rates, electricity or gas bills. They were thrifty and bought nothing they could not afford.

With such a big family, clothes were quite an important item in their budget. But we never wore second-hand clothes, except for the ones handed down in the family. We bought good quality clothes with generous hems and "turnings" so that they could be altered easily. I often fell heir to Betty's skirts and dresses, something I complained bitterly about sometimes. Jean was luckier. she often had to get new things because by the time two of us had used them they were only fit for the ragman to exchange for a balloon.

We always had special clothes for Sundays. Each Easter Sunday we went to Church and Sunday School wearing a new dress, coat and hat. Each winter, those who needed them had new warm coats to wear. We had a small stock of uniforms for Guides and Brownies which were passed down to me and Jean when our turn came.

As my parents were musical themselves, they never grudged the money spent on piano lessons. We all got a chance to take the opportunity or not as we felt inclined. I took that opportunity and never regretted it. I trudged along the front of the Links to my teacher's house every week for years. He charged 15/- a quarter (75 pence). I hated practising and only did it just before a lesson. In spite of that, I passed exams and received a good grounding in sight-reading which has been useful to me ever since.

We understood without question that there were some things we could not ask for. Mother and Dad believed in equal opportunities. Therefore if we asked for anything which, if you multiplied the cost by eight, would strain the family finances, we knew beforehand the answer would be "no". Sometimes we would push our luck and go on at some length about our request. This always irritated Mother so that when my Father came home he was greeted with, "Dad, will you speak to her? She's done nothing but "craik" all day". A word of two from him and the subject was closed.

In the years since their marriage my parents had built up a good standard of living for themselves and their children. No little effort had gone into it. By the time the three kids started school, we had absorbed by one means or another, the rules we were expected to keep both inside and outside the house. If we bothered to think about them in detail, they seemed perfectly reasonable to us.

CHAPTER 10

Learning the rules

I suppose my mother and father were quite strict parents but they were not at all unusual in the standards they set for us. All our chums, as far as we could tell, had the same kind of upbringing. The spadework my parents had put in with the first five children now brought its reward and to a great extent the teaching given to them was absorbed unconsciously by the three kids.

We were never lectured about right and wrong, well, hardly ever! But by a subtle process of suggestion and example, we were made aware of what was expected of us. We were also made aware that swift and sharp chastisement followed any misbehaviour. We made mistakes but we seldom made the same one twice. We soon found out either how to disguise them, or to take our punishment on legs or bottom!

Something which made it easier for parents was that there was no conflict with influences outside the home. All the organisations we joined so enthusiastically had the same aims. The first discipline we learned when we joined was the simple one of turning up on time on the right day each week. Then, when you had mastered that one, their rules were made perfectly clear. Some of the rules may seem laughable to modern children but they worked.

Another strong influence was our reading matter. We gobbled up an amazing amount of comics, magazines, newspapers, books both fiction and non-fiction. Then as films developed, we absorbed some of the mannerisms and conduct we saw on the screen. This cannot have been easy for parents as children began to use such American expressions as "scram", "oh yeah", "sez you" instead of "go away", "is that so?" and "I don't believe you!" But these were harmless variations of our vocabulary and soon accepted.

The relationship between parents and children then was that the parents provided food, clothes, shelter and in return they expected respect and obedience. The father was head of the house as the breadwinner and all the household arrangements centred on him. The mother controlled the purse strings and disciplined the children. As the children grew up and went out to work, they paid their contribution to the upkeep of the home and to a great extent they were expected to abide by the house rules until they married and left home. It was very unusual for a young person to leave home and set up a separate establishment before marriage.

In our case the house rules were simple. If you were late for a meal, the rest started without you. Borrowing each other's belongings without asking was taboo. Sulking after a quarrel, boasting, or showing off were discouraged. Quarrels of the "I did" "y' didn't" variety were stopped by the swift intervention of the referee, our mother. Coming in at night later than the time fixed for your age, unless with permission, merited a ticking off and if you pushed your luck and did it too often, a skelp on the lug reminded you to toe the line. We broke all these rules frequently. Practical rules which involved lack of consideration for other people were, no undue noise or playing the piano at unsocial hours, no thumping diabolos on the kitchen floor in case of annoying the neighbours down below. Unpunctuality was unforgivable. So was failing to do something you had promised to do.

We "came of age" at twenty-one years old. Traditionally, we were supposed to get the key of the front door on that birthday. In our case, all the time we lived in Woodbine Terrace, a key on a string was suspended from a hook behind the front door. You poked your forefinger through the letter box and pulled the key through. If you pulled too impatiently, it flew out and gave you sore fingers for your trouble! Everyone in our terrace knew that this was how we got into our house but we never thought of it as inviting a break-in. As far as we were concerned, burglars were those chaps in the comics with striped jerseys, masks and a sack over their shoulder with the word "SWAG" on it. We took it for granted that everyone was honest. We kept our illusions for quite a long time.

At Church and Sunday School it was impressed on us that God saw everything we did. This was embodied in a hymn we sang regularly

God is always near me,
Hearing what I say.
Knowing all my thoughts and deeds
All my work and play.

God is always near me,
Though so young and small.
Not a look or word or thought
But God knows it all.

What ominous words. They made us feel a bit uncomfortable until we forgot them! We did a great deal of hymn singing in those days, one way and another. The message was made clear. We had better be good, or we could go to the "burning fire". We gathered that punishment was inevitable, if not here, in the hereafter.

We were not "holy Willies" in our house. Grace was not said before meals and there were no Bible readings in the evenings. We said our prayers at bedtime when we were young but apart from that, our religious education was left to church and school. We were, however, expected to stick to Christian rules. We were constantly reminded to "Tell the truth and shame the Devil", sometimes a dangerous thing to do in our opinion since it frequently brought a skelp on the lug. "Have some consideration for other people", was a hard one too, if they did not appear to consider you. "Do unto others as you would be done by", another tough one to follow. If you came home with a tale of woe from school or work about an argument you had had with someone, Mother listened patiently and then said, "Try to think of the other person's point of view". This usually made us grind our teeth in fury, as that was the last thing we wanted to do!

Mother and Dad were the focal point of our family and they set us a very good example of how to get along in a small house. We never heard them arguing with each other, except in the most amicable and jocular way. If they had any more serious arguments they must have been conducted sotto voce in the privacy of their bedroom. Anything above that level would have been heard by us. We, of course, could make some racket at times as we were all great talkers, arguers, and fighters. If things got out of hand, we were told bluntly "Outside if you can't be quieter than that". As it is very difficult to conduct an acrimonious discussion in stage whispers for very long, if it was summer we went outside and it if was winter we shut up!

As with the older children, we learned that Mother had a way of administering discipline firmly and swiftly. She had no patience to spare if you complained of being punished at school and would just say "You must have deserved it"! Dad left all that to her, but if he gave us a telling off we trembled. On Saturdays after midday dinner, he liked to put his feet up on the fireplace, put a newspaper over his face and have an hour's snooze. We were expected to be quiet. If we made a noise, the feet would come down, the paper would be lowered and we would get a stern look with no word spoken. If we were very obstreperous, he would threaten us with "the belt". This was Dad's razor strop which hung just inside the scullery door and was made of fairly soft leather. He certainly never used it on us and it was only ever used to sharpen his cut-throat razor every day. It would not have hurt a fly.

They were very much against the "demon drink" and very seldom had any in the house, except at New Year time. Mother had seen her father the worse for drink in the past, so this was understandable. My father never went out to pubs in his life, I'm quite sure of that. As for his daughters, our environment was in his favour. No respectable woman went into a public house in Scotland, even if she had the money. They were very much of the spit and sawdust variety. I was over twenty-one years old before I even tasted whisky. All of us in turn joined the Band of Hope. We signed The Pledge and attended their meetings regularly where we sang songs about resisting the temptation of drink. One of them ran:-

> "Dare to be a Daniel;
> Dare to stand alone;
> Dare to pass a public house'
> And dare to make it known".

We had no clue as to what the words meant. In fact our Jim misinterpreted them completely for a long time. He thought the line "Dare to pass a public house" meant that he must not do that, as Mother used to say to him "don't you DARE" when he was about to do something she disapproved of. I went to the Band of Hope because you could buy for a penny, a bar of the most delicious tablet I have ever tasted.

I need hardly say we have all been cheerfully breaking The Pledge in moderation for many years, without too many ill-effects.

We were taught that waste was sinful and to be in debt unforgivable. "Neither a borrower nor a lender be" we were told. If we did borrow from each other, the debt had to be meticulously paid back to the last farthing. As for waste, nothing was thrown away which could be adapted to some other use. Our old vests and liberty bodices often turned up as washing or polishing cloths so that you felt you were cleaning the kitchen floor with an old friend! There was always some use for a handleless cup or a lidless teapot. Scraps of soap were saved up in a jam jar and used as soapy liquid for washing dishes. That was not popular with us. The mixed smells of the various soaps, acceptable one by one, were horrible put together. The paper in which butter, margarine or lard had been wrapped was carefully scraped. Even after that, it would be used for greasing a baking tray.

Buttons were removed from outworn clothes and kept in an old tea caddie for later use. Everyone we knew had a button box somewhere. Our clothes went through a recognisable transition; first as Sunday clothes then as everyday clothes and then they could be altered. A dress could be made into a skirt or a tired outfit could be brightened with a bit of trimming from Woolworths. We had a constant programme of make do and mend and were not ashamed to admit it. We only gave up when the thing was past redemption. Even now it hurts me to give away to a charity shop a perfectly good article for which I have no further use. I go through agonies of indecision before finally parting with it. The words "waste not, want not" were frequently heard in our house.

Sunday School for the three kids was much the same as it had been for the first five. The rules there of course were specific and inescapable. We were willing acolytes as they gave out lovely book prizes for good attendance. Off we went each Sunday dressed in our best, clutching our hymn book in one hand

and collection money in the other, to walk through the Links to St John's. Jim often played hookey quite shamelessly and left Jean and me at the start of the Links while he ran off to spend his collection money on high living wherever he could at that time on a Sunday. We never "clyped" on him. We knew that rule, and that it worked both ways!

An important part of our education was the glorification of various heroes and heroines of our time, or of times past. We knew all about Florence Nightingale the Lady with the Lamp, Nurse Cavell, Mary Slessor the Scottish missionary and Grace Darling, the lighthouse keeper's daughter who saved the lives of drowning men in heavy seas. My mother often told me that Grace had the same birthday as I had. Captain Scott's expedition to the South Pole was not very far in the past. We especially admired Captain Oates who went out of the tent to die in the snow in order to save his companions from the burden of his failing strength. How we loved all those stories of courage and endurance in the face of adversity. Many a time we beat a path to McDonald Road Library to take out books with stirring titles like, "Heroes of the Boer War", or "VCs of the Great War", or the epic battle of Rorke's Drift. It was intoxicating stuff which made you feel good to be part of the British Empire. We were unashamedly patriotic and proud not only of our British heritage, but of our own Scottish heritage. We loved romantic stories about the Jacobite Rebellion, Bonnie Prince Charlie and all that.

As well as all the historical heroes and heroines we had to choose from, there were the many fictional ones in comics and girls' and boys' magazines and annuals at Christmas time. They were mostly about young people at public schools having incredible adventures. We knew nothing about public schools but the adventures and heroic actions were what mattered. We liked a happy ending with the "goodies" triumphing over the "baddies" but if a heroic action meant a heroic death at the end, we approved of that, of course. Required reading at school was also of this order and the books dished out to us reinforced the teaching that right always prevailed over might and the goodies always won through in the end. We swallowed all of it willingly.

The youth organisations we joined had rules calculated to encourage us to toe the line and if you were a rebel, or failed to fit in, you just left. In the Brownies and the Guides we were expected to work at learning various skills to earn a "badge" which you sewed on to the sleeve of your tunic. The same system applied in the Scouts. There was a strict code of honour to follow. For instance, if you made a statement and added "Guide's honour" or "Scout's honour", you would be believed, as no one would imagine you would use that oath to support a lie.

The vow we made on joining the Guides was, "I promise on my honour to do my best, to do my duty to God and the King, to help other people at all times, and to obey the Guide Law". This "Law" was not to be treated lightly and was sternly specific in its demands on our behaviour. It read:-

A Guide's honour is to be trusted.
A Guide is loyal.
A Guide's duty is to be useful and to help others.
A Guide is a friend to all and a sister to
every other Guide.
A Guide is courteous.
A Guide is a friend to animals.
A Guide obeys orders.
A Guide smiles and sings under all difficulties.
A Guide is thrifty.
A Guide is pure in thought, word, and deed.

They were impossibly high ideals for all of us to fulfill all of the time but at least we tried some of the time. The one about smiling and singing made the most lasting impression on us. In our opinion, anyone who could smile and sing under all difficulties must have seriously failed to assess their difficulties accurately!

All of us spoke two languages. One for parents and teachers and one for our chums. We never mixed them up. We knew very well the rule about "no swearing", and stuck to it more or less. There was a vast area of swearing we knew nothing about. When I was about twelve years old I came home for midday dinner and took my seat at the table with Charlie, Jim and Betty, Mother presiding. I said, "Mother, what does 'fuck' mean?" Jim, who had just ladelled a spoonful of soup into his mouth, got such a shock that he spluttered soup all over the table. In the confusion, Mother managed to avoid giving me an answer but simply said, "Shut up and eat your soup". Something told me I had committed some dreadful gaffe and I obeyed instantly trying to hide my blushing face. The four letter words which are now bandied about in primary school playgrounds by lisping infants were unknown to us.

The strongest words my Mother ever used were "damn and blast", if she dropped a stitch in her knitting. Dad, when provoked, sometimes said "damnation". We were often told briskly to "go to the devil". On one occasion wee Mamie, thinking that it must be a good place to go, begged to be allowed to go too! We were ticked off for saying "heavens". Rude gestures were also frowned on and anyone caught poking a tongue out or thumbing a nose, got a clout from Mother's boney hands. We were all experts at what my father called "dumb insolence" but hardly ever got away with it.

There was a large area of fault which did not necessarily justify punishment and Mother and Dad had suitable catchphrases for all occasions. They were as familiar to us as the pattern on our kitchen wallpaper. When we did something silly, Mother cast her eyes heavenward and said "wae's me for Prince Chairlie". Bonnie Prince Charlie had not been in circulation in Scotland since the '45 rebellion. Who knows what forgotten ancient history that referred to. If we were helping Dad with anything and doing it badly, he would burst out with "Away you go, you're as much use as a hole in a doughnut!" That was better. We knew what a doughnut was! We were often told to stop hopping about "like a hen on a hot girdle", or if we were in the way, to "shift y'r barrie". Another of Dad's favourites was "God save Ireland". But the most ominous one was "and where d'ye think you've been till this time of night?!"

If Mother wanted one of us to fetch something for her she had a very cunning way of managing it. She would wait for one of us to rise from our seat, perhaps to go to the bathroom, and say very quickly, "while you're on your feet will you . . . " This would be followed by anything from "put the kettle on", "put some coal on the fire" to "run to the corner shop for a packet of salt". She was no fool, my mother!

We knew very little about sex. None of us was ever taken aside by Mother or Dad and told the "facts of life". Any knowledge we came by was gleaned from our school chums, or through the clandestine reading of magazines and books. There was no sex education at school. When we girls reached the age of puberty, we had to cope with the shock of menstruation in our own way. I was staying with my sister Madeline in Aberdeen when that happened to me. I expect I made a big fuss about it and eventually Madeline laughed and said, "Oh, shut up! It's not an illness you know". She was quite right. Ever since then I have managed to ignore it successfully. We had no knowledge of pre-menstrual tension either, that modern disease which is the excuse for so much bad behaviour.

When I got back from that holiday in Aberdeen, I felt it my duty to tell my mother of my new status. I chose a time when the two of us were walking up Lochend Road. I began my story but she was so obviously painfully embarrassed I gave up and had to face the fact that I could look for no guidance on such matters from her. Thank goodness for my older sisters who were not so inhibited. Even when we entered our teens and started going out with boys, we were given no guidance. Mother sometimes said, "Be careful" and gave us a meaning look. Be careful? What on earth did she mean? Did she mean "Don't get run over by a tram or bus?" We were utterly ignorant.

Our gleanings from books taught us that the safest way to deal with sex was to do without it until you married. Kissing and cuddling were safe enough but anything further was playing with fire. Of course, all the boys we knew had been brainwashed, in the same water as we had been, so it was never a problem. At the end of the day we were experts on love and romance but absolute beginners at sex.

The three kids had no thought of such matters when we started school at Hermitage Park but we had a good grounding in how to behave in public as well as at home. It was rude to contradict or interrupt elders. We must never let the family down. That was a difficult one to pin down. We must behave ourselves in school and do what the teacher told us. Most frightening of all, we were warned that if we misbehaved in class we would get "the belt".

Our five year old shoulders were not bowed down by all these "dos and don'ts" as we shrugged ourselves into our brand new leather schoolbags and set off, each in turn, to begin the long years of our education.

Jean, Jim and Nancy at Hermitage Park School, 1930

CHAPTER 11

Climbing up the twenties

Hermitage Park School was just up Lochend Road from us. My father said it had been jerry built. That puzzled me. Why would the Germans come over to Scotland to build a school for us? If I had consulted a dictionary I would have learned that it meant "constructed unsubstantially of bad materials". 'Hermy' still stands, outlasting many a more permanent-seeming building.

There were hutted classrooms in the playground and they had coke stoves for heating. So on cold winter mornings we sat steaming gently in our wet clothes amid the coke fumes. It's a wonder we survived!

The school building had a big hall with classrooms entered off the surrounding corridors. In the morning we gathered in the playground. There were separate playgrounds for boys and girls. Then a teacher appeared at the school door and rang a handbell. Quickly we arranged ourselves into lines and gradually quietened down as latecomers scuttled in just in time to avoid being late enough to earn punishment. To the sound of a stirring march on the piano by one of the teachers, we marched into school and peeled off into our classrooms. Often the march was a piece called "Marche aux Flambeaux". When I hear it now it never fails to remind me of the dusty smell of chalk on blackboard and the sights and sounds of Hermitage Park School.

Our teachers were strict and had no favourites. The lady who taught us in the qualifying class was a lovely person and we all liked her. She was probably in her late twenties but we thought of her as old, of course. She had a nice round face and a nice round body to go with it. She could control her classes with a casual glance over her shoulder. I cannot remember her ever having to raise her voice to us. She left to get married at the same time as we left to go to secondary school. We gave her a party and I presented her with a suitcase on behalf of the class. I had to make a little speech and I was very nervous I remember.

In the infants class, of course, there was more play than work when we first started but soon we were issued with wooden framed slates and slate pencils to write on them. I can never forget the resultant blood curdling squeaks of pencil on slates. It was a relief when we graduated to notebooks and lead pencils. Daily we recited our multiplication tables starting with the "two times" and slowly working up to the "twelve times". From there we progressed to multiplication, addition, short division and long division sums. We had regular tests in written and mental arithmetic. At first, mental arithmetic was a great trial to me, as the thought of having a time limit and no paper and pencil sent my brains flying out of the window but in time I managed to discipline my nerves to do quite well at it.

Spelling, reading and writing were more up my street. Eventually we were issued with copying books and real wet ink to copy laboriously the copperplate "joined up" writing as well as we could, thin upstrokes and broad downstrokes. There was a great deal of spluttering of pen nibs, frowning concentration and tongues poked out. Of course, we did homework as well, a few sums of the kind we were working on at the time; a dozen or so spelling words; a page or two of reading. In our house we did our homework sitting round the kitchen table in the early evening after tea, while the life of the house went on around us.

As soon as I learned to read fairly fluently, I had the key to a new world. I read everything that came my way from Force packets and H.P. sauce bottles to children's classics. This was an established family trait. My older sisters and brothers read voraciously. We all joined the public library as soon as we could. We read on trams, buses, at the table if we could get away with it, on foot walking up Lochend Road with a book in front of our noses, under the bedclothes at night with a torch. Our reading in the family ranged from fairy stories and myths of ancient Greece, to novels by H. Rider Haggard, Dickens, A.J. Cronin, Ethel M. Dell, D.K. Broster, Vicki Baum, John Buchan, Upton Sinclair, and later on, the crime novels of Leslie Charteris and Mickey Spillane. It stood us in good stead when it came to writing essays and we all enjoyed doing that in school.

Discipline at Hermitage Park was firm but if you did your work and behaved yourself there was no problem. I learned early to keep a low profile and as I was seldom absent and never late, I had no occasion to be punished.

The headmaster at Hermy I remember best was a big, bluff, jolly man, rather like a friendly gorilla. I expect he could be quite fierce when he was angry but thank goodness, I never saw him that way!

Silence was something our teachers valued. We frequently had to sit with our hands on our heads, or arms folded, for what seemed like hours. It was probably only a couple of minutes. Certainly not long enough for the blood to be cut off from our arms! The teachers had complete control and power over us poor mortals. Fortunately for us, they never seriously abused their power. They allotted us places in the classroom which we won according to our marks in the most recent test or examination. There were no hangups about the less able pupil feeling embarrassment at being seated at the front and the clever ones at the back. It was impressed on us that we all had the opportunity to be at the top if we worked hard. That was life.

As far as I know, my brothers and sisters all did very well at school and were in the top sections of their classes. The reason I know so little about it is that bragging about such things was not looked on kindly in our family and was likely to get loud "raspberries" all round. We were not under a lot of pressure as some children are today. If the report cards had a good sprinkling of "V.G." and "Excellent" for the subjects and behaviour in class, Mother and Dad were satisfied. If we won a prize or two that was a bonus.

There were no students' grants to look forward to, and with eight children to provide for, unless one of us turned out to be a juvenile Einstein, university was not our goal. All the first five passed the "Quali." without any trouble and went on to Leith Academy. It was a fee-paying school at that time. All, that is, except our Mamie. She passed the Quali. alright but she and some of her chums decided they would not go to Leith Academy but to Bonnington Road School, just to be different. Needless to say, all her chums reneged, and Mamie ended up as the only one who went to Bonnington Road. She came to terms with that and finished her schooling there without any problem. We were all encouraged to face up to and conquer our own difficulties and get on with it. So she did. As for myself, at the risk of loud raspberries but in the interest of truth, I gained $97^1/_2$% in the Quali. and still have the book I won on that occasion.

Other activities apart from the three Rs, history and geography, were singing, sport, including swimming, knitting and sewing. The songs we sang,and which my own children were still singing twenty-five years later, were "A flaxen headed cowboy", "Early one morning", "Sailing down to Rio", "Soldier soldier won't you marry me?', "Golden slumbers".

As for sport, we played overhead ball with great determination and I enjoyed the competitive spirit of that. Most of all, I loved running in the flat races and often won. Our Sports Day took place at Hawkhill sports ground, and for weeks beforehand, we practised the three-legged race up and down the terrace, or the egg and spoon race, with a stone for the egg. Once a week when we were a little older, we were escorted as a class to Dr Bell's School Baths. I have no memory of any tuition there. I taught myself to swim on picnics to the seaside, starting in very shallow water until I was confident enough to venture further into deeper waters.

Sewing and knitting were not my favourite subjects. We all had to make our own sewing bag. This consisted of a kind of apron with a big pocket to keep our work in which you tied round your waist. We practised hemming, tacking, oversewing quite laboriously but nothing really useful ever came of it. My knitting was very poor as well. I had absolutely no enthusiasm for it. As far as I was concerned it was all a waste of time.

In the playground, we played a lot of strenuous games, some of them very dangerous. We had permanently scarred knees from falling and scabby elbows as well. In the winter when the ground had icy snow on it, we made long slides in the playground. There were slides everywhere you looked, running into each other, running across each other, the whole length and breadth of the playground. With the confidence of unthinking youth, we set off down a slide, barely missing other sliders along the way, miraculously arriving at the railing unscathed. We expected to, and did! Just occasionally, if that kind of weather persisted for a few days and the pond in Lochend Park was frozen, a rumour would go round that we would get a "skating holiday" in the afternoon. After a few tantalising days we would be told we could have the afternoon off for skating or sledging. Those who were lucky enough to own or be able to borrow ice-skates or sleds, went off to find suitable places. The thought of skating on the pond in Lochend Park did not attract us, as we had always been told that it was bottomless, and that a horse and cart had once driven into it never to be seen again. We had no wish to join them. But perhaps this was a story put about by parents to deter children from skating on thin ice. Instead, we went sliding or snowballing, deserting the school playground to make long slides down Lochend Road. Occasionally there was a bit of excitement if a horse fell while climbing the hill of Lochend Road. The word went round quickly, so that the poor beast had an audience as it lay shivering and shaking with fear while its master tried to get it back on its feet with the help of any ablebodied men who happened to be around and copious advice from bystanders. Those of us with tender feelings for the horse did not wait to see the end of the story.

There was one playground drama which took place every morning at playtime. Betty, who had another year to do at Hermy when I started there, used to seek me out and pinch half the buttered roll I always took with me for a playpiece. Somehow I never learned to hide from her. She was a lot bigger than me so I made no protest, but often cast it up to her later on!

I cannot leave my memories of Hermitage Park School without mentioning special occasions there, some of them associated with breaking up for Easter, Christmas or summer holidays. These were all happy events for which we practised hymns, carols, choir singing, solos if you could play an instrument, or recite a poem. There was a happy relaxation of discipline prior to the holidays and we often found our teachers, to our surprise and delight, could be just like children themselves. A record which our teacher used to play to us as a special treat at such times was called "The Laughing Policeman", sung by Charles Penrose. Nothing is so infectious as laughter so we were soon helpless with mirth, our teacher in the same state, just as daft as us! Released at the end of term, we went home to enjoy the special treats which represented Christmas, or to prepare hard boiled, decorated eggs to roll own the Giant's Brae in Leith Links at Easter time.

One very important yearly event in the twenties and thirties was Remembrance Day held to commemorate the signing of the Armistice on 11th November 1918 at 11.00 am. Emotions regarding the loss of loved ones in the Great War were still very sensitive. The three kids, of course, were children of the post-war period but by the time we went to school, we had learned from our parents that the Great War had been a terrible time for them. Our Uncle Jimmy had been killed in France before we were born. We knew every line of Jimmy's face and uniform from long and wondering study of his photograph. We sang all the sad sounding wartime songs associated with that war. "Roses are blooming in Picardy", "There's a long long trail awinding", and "Keep the home fires burning", were part of our lives. Sometimes while singing them you had a lump in your throat without knowing why.

Dad used to sing a song which began:-

Trumpeter, what are you sounding now?
Is it the call I'm seeking?

and later went on:-

Lucky for you if you hear it at all,
As my trumpet goes aseeking.
I'm calling them home, come home, come home.
Tread light on the dead in the valley,
Who are lying around face down on the ground . . .

What pictures, however inaccurate, that conjured up for us.

All over Britain in schools and churches in those years, Armistice Day was an important day of remembrance. During the preceding fortnight, Earl Haig poppies were on sale in the streets, in shops, in schools, and door-to-door. The simple poppy by itself cost a penny, but for 3d or 6d, you could buy a more elaborate one with a bit of imitation greenery.

On the day, our teacher reminded us of the sacrifice made by the men killed and maimed in the Great War. We listened, wide eyed and ignorant, trying to grasp the enormity of such a state of affairs where men's lives were at such risk not by accident, but by calculation.

At 11 am we all sat silent for two minutes with our heads bowed. We knew that in Edinburgh and Leith, indeed all over Britain, cars, buses, tramcars, horse-drawn traffic, pedestrians, men with bared heads bowed and women at work or in their own homes, nothing moved for those two minutes. Any insensitive person who did not observe this would soon be made aware that he might be physically injured if he failed to pay respect to the dead. In shops, public offices and banks, it was as if all had been turned to stone. Anyone in a hurry to be served was out of luck. Even if you were alone in a room, those two thoughtful minutes were observed.

Later that morning we walked in our classes to a local church where we sang emotional and patriotic hymns, "I vow to thee my country", "Onward Christian soldiers", or "Soldiers of Christ arise" and listened to the minister's sermon about courage and sacrifice.

What could we know of such things at our age? We knew nothing. But there was a message there we understood instinctively and none of us treated the occasion lightly.

Those of us who were involved with movements such as Guides or Scouts, and at one time or another that meant most of the Harrises, had a further ceremony on the Sunday nearest to Armistice Day. All the churches had a special service then. We formed up outside Pattison Street Hall with the Guides. We had two colour parties, one with the Company flag, and one with the Union flag. Then we marched to St John's. When all the congregation was assembled, the colour parties and the rest of the parade took their places, one at the top of each aisle. To the singing of "O God of Bethel" the two colour parties set off down each aisle. The minister received the flags and placed them on either side of the communion table which was decorated with poppies. There they remained for the duration of the service. It was a great honour to be chosen to be either carrier of the flag, or one of the two supporters in these colour parties, and over the years the Harris family was well represented. The flags were quite heavy and I recall vividly how embarrassed I was when the tip of mine rattled on the underside of the gallery! What a red face I had! After the service the colours were carried out with equal ceremony and we formed up outside the church with an interested assembly of the congregation, including our parents, to march back to the hall in Pattison Street.

For the rest of the church and school year, these gloomy matters did not exercise our minds very much as our history books never included the period of the Great War. It was still too painful a subject. We thought no more about it until the following year.

Although I enjoyed school, the holidays were always welcomed. They were spent by us in indefatigable pursuance of games like kick-the-can, Araleevoi, rounders, peevers, diabolo, spinning peeries, tig, hide 'n' seek, all games which could be played by both boys and girls. Skipping rope games were for the lassies, and more tranquil pastimes for them were crocheting and knitting for our dolls, or collecting and swapping "scraps".

We laid out our "peevery beds" with white chalk on the paving stones. Most of the peevers we used were empty tins. Mansion Polish tins were in great demand. Even now I find myself sizing up a tin's potential as a peever, although they have almost vanished from the supermarket shelves to be replaced by spray cans. Not useful at all. The best kind of peever was a smooth, round piece of polished marble. They slid easily when they were tapped as you hopped on one leg. They were difficult to come by unless you knew a stonemason.

Jean and I had lovely diabolos. They were made by father and were perfectly balanced. We were adept at throwing them high into the air and catching them on the taut string attached to two sticks held in our hands. It needed great skill but once you got the hang of it, as long as your eyesight was good, it was a fascinating pastime.

We loved to whip our peeries into a state of "sleeping" and the trick was in keeping them that way as long as you could. Ball games, of course, were always popular if someone happened to own a ball. The owner of the ball had the ball at his feet, so to speak. He or she was quite likely to end the game abruptly with "it's ma baw, an' am no' playin'!"

Sometimes we invested in a wee clay pipe and with soapy water blew bubbles. We were never allowed to do that in the house because it was such a "slaister".

The skipping ropes we used were usually pieces from an old washing line, the longer the better so you could cram more people in to skip in the middle. Then there were skipping rhymes you could chant like "salt, pepper, mustard, vinegar" while you skipped faster and faster. We carried in our heads a vast repertoire of chants and rhymes, along with the sometimes complicated rules of the games with which they were associated. Some of them I have quoted as an appendix to this book. They were compiled by James T.R. Ritchie for his books *The Singing Street* and *Golden City*, published by Oliver and Boyd.

When we were old enough, Jean and I got scooters for Christmas and we loved them. To us it was like flying. We had iron girds and cleiks as well. The exhilaration of running down Lochend Road with a gird in front of you has never been surpassed for me, even by driving a car. The only bicycles in our family were for practical purposes and not for fun. My father, Netta, Charlie, and Jim each had one to get them to work. We found our own way of learning how to ride a bike. We begged a "shot" on a friend's, and once you learn you never forget.

In the summer, we went to Portobello beach for picnics, or up to the King's Park to romp around the grass, or climb Arthur's Seat. Our days were very full. When it was hot and the tar blistered and bubbled on Lochend Road, we loved to burst the bubbles with our bare toes. The smell of the hot tar was very intoxicating, but we got a severe telling off if we went home with tar anywhere on our clothes! It was so difficult to clean off. The words "bored" or "fed up" were not very often heard. If we showed signs of drooping around the house our mother, after checking our temperature by putting her hand on our forehead, told us to go and find something to do. "Get out from under my feet" she would say in exasperation.

Our outside stair had its uses. We used to "dreep" from varying heights to the ground below. Sometimes we sat on the railing which surrounded the top step with a drop of about twenty feet below us. Or we would see how many steps we could jump down, constantly trying to better our performance as we got taller. With hindsight, some of our pastimes were jolly dangerous. We were very seldom taken to task on that score. Taking risks was all part of childhood and a "skint knee" or two was never a drama.

We sometimes slid down our inside carpeted stair lying on our stomachs, controlling our speed with our hands. If you lost control you were in trouble. On one occasion, Jean fell down the stairs. With an astonished howl of anguish, I threw myself after her in sympathy, practically landing on top of her. By a miracle no bones were broken.

We were friendly with the children of the janitor of St Anthony's School. They lived in the house attached to the school. The deserted playground was a great place for us to play. In one of the sheds there was a ladder stored in the roof with the odd rung missing. We used to swing along it hand over hand, like monkeys. It was in the janitor's house that I learned to stand on my hands, my feet resting on a door. The first time I tried it, I collapsed on my head. I had not realised that you have to practice and build up the strength in your arms for a while until they can support your weight. I suppose we were rather tomboyish. We had a go at most of the things the boys did. Guiders, roller skates, handstands, various rough ball games, bools, climbing and dreeping, we tried them all.

When the weather forced us to find pastimes indoors, we had plenty of choice. The old favourite board games and playing cards were still very popular but we girls had our own special games such as "scraps". For a small outlay, we could buy a sheet of them from Young's with colourful representations of angels, baskets of flowers, crinolined ladies, shepherd boys and girls on them. We separated them from each other, placed them between the leaves of a book or in a chocolate box, and we were in the business of swapping scraps. The chocolate boxes then were very sturdy and able to take a lot of handling before they fell to bits. They were often things of beauty, to be admired and coveted. They could be treasured for many years without disintegrating. We increased our stock of scraps by buying a few each week with a precious Saturday penny, and if you were careful, when the time for scraps was past, they were still there the following year. We certainly never foresaw a year when these things would not come round in their turn.

We had many games played with pencil and paper. They were educational, of course, but if anyone had suggested that to us, we would have been very surprised. One was called simply "Bird, Beast". A group would decide on a letter of the alphabet and then you wrote down as many birds, beasts and flowers you could think of beginning with that letter. Whoever had the most won. There were no prizes. Only the satisfaction of winning.

Another absorbing paper and pencil game was Dot-to-dot, which involved setting out dots to form small squares. You took it in turn to join up the dots and when you completed all four sides of a square, you put your initials in it to show your ownership. The one with most initials won the game. The other aim was to stop your opponents from completing squares on the same principle as noughts and crosses which we also played quite a lot. Consequences was another popular game we played, especially at parties.

Cutting out paper dolls and dressing them was always a fascinating occupation. You could buy paper dolls with clothes to cut out, but we drew our own dolls and cut them out. Then we drew dresses, coats and hats, underwear, and shoes, all with little tabs to fix them to the dolls. Sometimes we found a suitable magazine with pictures to cut out, or to give us ideas for clothes. I still cast a professional eye over those pattern books in the shops and think they would be great for cut outs. Again, a sturdy chocolate box was ideal for keeping our work in.

We often went round the local shops asking for "any empty boxes" and it was amazing what you could make of them, depending on your imagination; beds for dolls, buses, trams, prams, forts, castles, thrones, pulpits, shops.

Knitting and crocheting were popular. We did that with no particular idea in mind, so our work often ended by being a dog's or doll's blanket. I was not particularly good at it. My older sisters used to crochet the most beautiful berets for themselves in lovely colours. They were very fashionable in the twenties. We also made "reins", using an empty pirn with four small nails driven into the top. The knitted "rope" came through the bottom. It was quite a soothing occupation but I never yet saw any reins made by that method, and conclude that the means was the end as well!

Some Sunday evenings while Mother and Dad were at church, we used to roast potatoes in the open fire. We lifted them out with the fire tongs when we thought they were ready. They were usually quite black, but we loved them, including the black bits. Also on a Sunday evening Jim, who fancied himself as an orator, used to upend the big wooden stool we had, turning it into a pulpit, and we got an impromptu sermon. We listened rather inattentively, but we liked singing the hymns. Thank goodness he grew out of that.

Many a Sunday evening was spent sitting round the kitchen fire singing. We had no accompaniment, but from an early age most of us could sing harmonies. We did not scorn simple musical instruments like the Jew's harp, the kazoo, or tissue paper and comb which tickled our lips. We sang all the old students' songs, Gilbert and Sullivan, popular music hall songs and songs from the films we saw.

Before Jim was banished from the big bedroom as being too old to be among all the girls, we three kids had our own games played after lights out. These were word games like, "The Minister's Cat", or, "I spy with my little eye". We had one where one of us tapped out a tune on the wall and the other two had to guess what the tune was. By that time, in winter, we were privileged to have an Aladdin paraffin lamp in the middle of the floor. We played our games gazing at the interesting pattern the lamp cast on the ceiling until, one after another, we dropped off to sleep.

Jim used to enjoy telling me and Jean ghost stories. He even acted them out with the help of a sheet and much moaning and groaning. Jean used to squeak and squawk in terror and hide under the bedclothes. He never fooled me. I knew it was just Jim!

On one or two occasions, Jean and I were taken down to Dad's James Lane workshop, probably to allow my mother to go out somewhere without us. It was a huge place to us, full of mysteries and magical surprises. We loved running up and down the office stairs, or watching the men sawing planks of wood on the machine saw which whined noisily. Safety rules were not very strict then but we knew to keep a respectful distance. We only had to look at Dad's fingers to know what machinery could do. He had had one or two little accidents which made his hands more interesting than anybody else's.

We used to climb among the big planks of wood stacked to the ceiling, or watch the wee pots of glue melting on top of the coal fired stove. Its chimney went up through the roof, and we were forbidden to touch it as it was hot. We loved to play at shops. What a fund of variety we could have with fine sawdust for flour, coarser sawdust for sugar, wedges of wood for cheese, and square pieces for butter. Putty, in a manner of speaking, was meat and drink to us. We could make potatoes with it. Sometimes we took a little home to play with until the oil dried out and we threw it away. The big curly shavings we used to attach to our own hair as ringlets and curls. Netta sometimes allowed us to have a go with her typewriter but only while she watched us. Her Smith Premier, with its double keyboard is still in our family and usable, although not in use.

During these years in the twenties, I suppose we three got more attention than the first five. We had no complaints. The older ones never grudged us the nice clothes and frequent treats we had, owing to Dad's success in business. They seemed very old to us. Betty left school in 1929, the day she became fourteen years old, so there was quite a gulf between the first five and the three kids. The gap lessened as we got older. Unfortunately, that year brought to Mother a health crisis which was to cast a shadow over the rest of her life. With such a houseful of people to look after, her life was one long round of work. It is no wonder that her energy began to flag. Each day her work seemed to demand more and more effort from her. Dad engaged a woman to come on a Monday morning to do the washing, at a cost of 3/6d (18 pence), and the older girls were roped in to wash dishes, do the ironing, and help prepare meals.

In spite of their efforts, Mother's health began to give serious concern. Our doctor advised that she should get away for two weeks for a rest. He arranged for her to go to a "home for tired mothers", in Galashiels. So that summer, taking Jean, who was six years old, with her, she left us to take care of each other while she rested at the Home. She was forty-four years old, worn down by constant childbearing and hard work. Instead of the carefree rest she expected, she became seriously ill with pneumonia, the same illness which had claimed her father's life. Word was sent to my father and a few anxious days went by. Fortunately, Mother survived the crisis point of her illness and began to recover. She was weak and helpless but she was on the mend. We three kids had no idea that our mother had been fighting for her life. We only heard of it when we were older. Dad took me to Galashiels to visit her. She lay in bed, too weak to sit up, looking very thin and peelie-wallie. During this time, wee Jean was left to droop about the Home watching the chambermaids at their work, or the dining room staff laying tables. She remembers it as a very unhappy time.

At home, we all had to help in the house in Mother's absence. Some strange concoctions we ate, according to our sisters' tastes. Even Jim was kept busy. He obligingly made a jelly one day for dessert. He dropped it on the floor and had to chase it around to recapture it. He served it to us without a word. No one noticed anything wrong.

When we got the good news that Mother was well enough to come home, there was a perfect frenzy of cleaning. The kitchen floor was scrubbed with plenty of elbow grease, and polished with Mansion Polish. The furniture shone, the washing and ironing were up to date, and everything was spick and span.

She came home in a taxi all the way from Galashiels. A TAXI! That was a form of transport we never used if there was a bus, tram or train. If she had come home on an elephant, we could not have been more surprised. She was so weak she could not enjoy her taxi ride and she lay along the seat with Jean sitting on the floor beside her.

It was a long time before she was well enough to begin taking back the reins of the household. She appeared to return to normal, but it was from that time that her health imperceptibly deteriorated, and each winter she was laid low with bronchitis.

It was from that time also that we all had to give some help with the work of the household. Sad to say we were often "pressed men" rather than volunteers. With the selfishness of youth, we sometimes tried to wriggle out of our duties. There were arguments about whose turn it was to do the dishes after tea. "It's your turn", "No, it's not. It's your turn", we would go on and on about it. Usually Dad had to be the referee and his decision was final.

As we brought in the year 1930 in traditional fashion, none of us yet realised that our mother had a health problem from which she would never really recover. My father's business was doing very well — in his mid-forties now, he was a respected businessman and happy in his work. His first five children were all working; the three kids were at school. The family unit was still intact. No war nor rumour of war disturbed us and we had no fears for the future.

Nancy, Jim, Madeline, Jean, 1933

CHAPTER 12

Plunging into the thirties

The 1930s brought many changes. Motor traffic had increased and it was no longer so safe to play in the middle of the road. Even in the terraces we had to keep a sharp eye open for the occasional car or lorry. We were quite used to aeroplanes but they were still rare enough to make us look up when we heard one and chant "an aeroplane an aeroplane, fifty miles and back again!" The possibility that we ourselves might be hopping onto 'planes and travelling around the world in them never occurred to us.

Telephones had been in use for a long time for business purposes and were spreading to private houses but we knew no one who had a telephone. If we had to make a call, we went to the wee shop at the corner. It had a 'phone and we paid the shopkeeper for the call. If we had urgent news to send, we could send a telegram. That means of conveying news had a bad reputation from the days of the war when it always brought bad news. We avoided it if we could, in case the recipient had a heart attack before he even read the telegram!

Some lucky householders had washing machines but we did not even know of their existence. The Hoover carpet sweeper had come to Britain and it took hold quickly. What an improvement that was on the laborious business of switching the carpets with a stiff brush on hands and knees.

More and more the emphasis was on leisure and there were plenty of ways to occupy us in our free time. Each weekend the cities were deserted, as young and old took to the hills, valleys and the seaside by whatever means in their power. Bicycling clubs were very popular. It was something to see these large companies of cyclists going past in twos, dressed in shorts and Aertex shirts, bent over their machines and pedalling away like mad. At first glance you would be unable to tell the difference between the men and the women. They all dressed the same. The young girls very often had an Eton crop which made them look more like boys than the boys did!

Then there were the hiking clubs which took to the road in all kinds of dress. Bent under the weight of their rucksacks, they tramped the country roads and hills, usually singing the hikers' national anthem "I'm happy when I'm hiking". It was from these clubs that the Youth Hostel movement developed which became, and still is, such a wonderfully inexpensive way to have a holiday. The Y.M.C.A. and the Y.W.C.A., hobbies and rambling clubs flourished too. Several members of our family were involved with a motor cycling club which had regular weekend fixtures in the summer, dances and other functions in winter. All these organisations brought young people together socially and many a romance resulted from them.

A popular movement of that time was the Women's League of Health and Beauty, with Prunella Stack at its head. All over Britain, girls were encouraged to exercise in order to be healthy and beautiful. The aim was to acquire a "good figure", whatever that may mean. No longer were the bustless and hipless figures of the twenties popular. A good bust was important, a neat waist, hips not too large, and an upright figure. In fact, if they had known there would be women in the Forces within a few years, they could not have done a better job. My older sisters often did their exercises before going to bed and they used to pore over the health and beauty magazines. These contained photographs of scantily dressed girls in athletic poses. By no stretch of the imagination could you describe these magazines as "girlie". The reproductions were in black and white and the models were rather po-faced; certainly not sexually provocative. Perish the thought!

One of the great influences on us was the wireless which had quickly become common in many households after the first broadcast in 1922. The receiver was most likely to have been put together by the family enthusiast, working at it into the small hours. What a thrill when he could "get" Hilversum or Radio Luxembourg. By the end of the decade a wireless and a gramophone were practically standard equipment in the home, especially where there were young people.

My father embraced both these inventions with enthusiasm. In Pirniefield days, he once brought home a second-hand wind-up gramophone with a few records and sat up till three o'clock in the morning playing them over and over again.

At Woodbine, we had a more up-to-date model in a lovely wooden cabinet in our parlour. It was a magical invention to us. If we failed to keep it wound up, it groaned to a grinding halt and there was a mad rush to ca' the handle. The needles had to be changed regularly, otherwise you got a very scratchy result. My parents bought the records of the tuneful popular music they loved. We had "The Belle of New York", "Miss Hook of Holland", and overtures like "The Merry Wives of Windsor", and "William Tell". They also liked monologues and songs by Will Fyffe and Harry Gordon. We knew them by heart. My sisters built up their own collection of records when they began earning. Jazz and smoochy love ballads were their favourites. Dad did not always approve of their choice. He thought some of the lyrics were suggestive. In the case of one particular record he drew the line. It was called "Body and Soul" which went:-

My heart is sad and lonely.
I sigh for you, for you dear only.
Why haven't you seen it?
I'm all for you body and soul.

Dad broke that record over his knee in disgust. We had absolutely no idea why! We all knew the words and sang them over and over again, but their implication was lost on us. Another one included the words:-

Oh, I can't break away,
I must have you every day,
As regularly as coffee or tea.
You've got me in your clutches
And I can't break free,
You're getting to be a habit with me!

The words seem tame now compared with the pop songs of today with their suggestions of drugs and sex.

Years ago my father had built our first cat's whisker wireless set from the printed circuits available. We had to put on earphones to hear it. Then there were two later models but eventually we bought a very handsome set with a fretwork design on the front to cover the speaker. We were enthusiastic listeners to the dance bands and crooners. We were eager learners and there was so much to learn. Happy songs, sad songs, we loved them all. "Happy days are here again" and "I want to be happy" were very popular. Equally, we enjoyed a good wallow with "All alone by the telephone", "Say it isn't so", "What'll I do?" The tenor voice of Richard Tauber singing "You are my heart's delight", or the rich bass voice of Paul Robeson singing "Ole man river" seem to encapsulate the mood of that time. The film of the musical "Rose Marie", with Nelson Eddy and Jeanette MacDonald, came to Edinburgh and we were soon all singing and whistling the "Indian Love Call". Our parents must have been deeved to death with that one.

There is no doubt that wireless and films were a considerable influence on our generation as well as my father's. Poor Dad had to accept that he could no longer control the torrents of words and music which entered our house with the turn of a switch. We absorbed everything. All kinds of music, plays, and talks. The names and voices of a wide range of radio personalities were instantly recognisable to us at their first word. We could identify each of the dance bands by their signature tunes, or by their style of musical arrangement. We soaked up a vast repertoire of music, light and classical, like dry sponges. They satisfied in us a hunger and thirst we had not known we had. Mother and Dad, in spite of this bombardment, never took to Wagner or Brahms or chamber music. They stuck to their own choice. They knew what they liked.

We often bought the sheet music for some of our favourite numbers so that we could have a piano accompaniment. The covers of these pieces of music were often works of art, with details of the band and singer who first made them famous.

There is one more pastime which greatly influenced us, and that was "going to the pictures". The development of the film industry brought us a form of entertainment which had spread all over the world. Made in America, those early films allowed us to see very different ways of life. In the early twenties we saw

Charlie Chaplin, Harold Lloyd, Fatty Arbuckle and Ben Turpin. They were silent films, all with the aim of making us laugh. They did! The overworked pianist in the orchestra pit, thumped away to provide a musical background. Then when the "talkies" arrived in Edinburgh and Leith in 1929, "going to the pictures" increasingly became a once a week or, if the programme changed midweek, twice a week habit for everyone with the price of admission.

The Capitol Cinema in Manderston Street which opened in 1928, was our local. Dad and Mother loved an evening at the "Capi" now that their older family could look after the younger ones while they were out. Most of the films were suitable for children and we often queued for an hour or more to see our favourites on a Saturday afternoon. If we got in before four o'clock, it cost only fourpence (less than 2 pence). If it was House Full, it was up to the uniformed commissionaire at the door to let you in when two or three members of the audience came out. When he graciously motioned you forward, you bought your ticket at the box office. Then you handed it to the usherette to be torn in half and have your half returned to you. You plunged into the darkness of the auditorium to be taken over by another usherette who conducted you to your seat with the help of her torch. As soon as you sat down, your eyes were on the screen. Sometimes you found yourself in one of the side seats in the front stalls, the worst ones in the whole auditorium. From there, the images on the screen were curiously elongated and distorted. So were your neck muscles because of the nearness of the screen. You watched the film while keeping a weather eye open for a better seat, and when you saw your opportunity, you made your move.

If the big picture had started, you just had to follow the drift of the plot as best you could. Then between the main feature and the 'B' picture, the lights went up and the icecream and sweet sellers made their rounds. Sometimes a sing-song would follow. The cinema organ rose out of the orchestra pit with the organist playing his "signature tune". Community singing over, the organ disappeared again, and the lights dimmed. The curtains parted to reveal the certificate issued by the Board of Censors and the music began to set the mood of the film. We stopped rustling the sweetie papers and concentrated on the plot. After the 'B' film there might be a "Silly Symphony", a newsreel, and a "trailer" for the following week's programme. If you had gone in in the middle of the big picture, you had seen the end before you saw the beginning, so when you began to recognise scenes you had already seen, it was time to leave. Where you came in determined when you came out and you had had your money's worth without a doubt.

We had our favourite film stars and fell in and out of love with them frequently. I was madly in love with Robert Taylor for at least three weeks, until Ronald Colman or someone else took his place. We did our best to look like the female stars we admired. Clara Bow, Lilian Harvey, Ruby Keeler, Elissa Landi and Marion Davis were our idols in the early thirties. We copied their hairstyles and makeup. Their cupid's bow lips were superimposed on our natural lips with lipstick. We plucked our thick youthful eyebrows, and Vaselined our eyelids to give them that smouldering look. Film stars' clothes were discussed endlessly and copied as faithfully as we could. After the straight fashions of the twenties, a more romantic and flattering style of dress began to emerge under the influence of these ladies.

Films influenced us in other ways too. These Americans we saw on the screen seemed to live in luxury. They had refrigerators, washing machines, dish washers, air conditioning, central heating, things we had never heard of. They were well ahead of us and we would have to hurry to catch up with them. It appeared to be a strange new world and we were eager to learn.

Almost as enjoyable as a good laugh at the pictures, we loved a "good greet". If it was the last showing of the evening, the lights went up, and the hankies were furtively put away while we stood for God Save the King. Then we stumbled out through a mist of tears!

We loved to be frightened as well. Bela Lugosi, Lon Chaney and King Kong drew the crowds night after night. These were the days when the name "Dracula" sent a shiver down your spine. When King Kong was showing in one cinema, the management offered a reward to anyone who would sit and watch it alone in the cinema starting at midnight. Nowadays when I see that film on TV, it strikes me that King Kong was just a great big pussycat. He seems to get more sympathy than Fay Wray, the heroine.

These years in the early thirties gave my parents a kind of freedom they had never tasted before. Now in their mid-forties, both of them had worked hard and singlemindedly to achieve the benefits our family now enjoyed. It is at this time in their lives that I have the most vivid impression of them. My father had built up his business from nothing and was respected as a man of honesty and integrity. He never expected his tradesmen to do anything he could not do himself, and his apprentices had an excellent grounding in their trade. My brother Charlie, now over twenty-one, had been his first apprentice. He was working now as a journeyman for another firm. It was expected that Jim, in his turn, would follow Charlie's example when he reached the age of fourteen.

We were sometimes drawn into his business affairs. It was usual for firms to send out as a gift to their regular customers, a calendar at Christmas time, and Dad was no exception. We enjoyed taking part in the selection of the picture for the calendar. Usually it was a very traditional one, with huntsmen in red coats drinking ale round a blazing fire or a lively Christmas scene. It is a way of advertising which has largely died out now.

To us, as well as being our Dad and therefore utterly taken for granted by us, he was as solid and reliable as anyone could be. You could set your watch by the times he went out in the mornings to work, came back for midday dinner, went back in the afternoon, and came back in the evening. We knew his step at the door. He always threw his cap with unerring accuracy on to the hallstand as he came in.

He was the one who bound up our wounds, mended broken toys, sharpened our pencils, peeled our oranges, and had the last say in anything important we wanted to do. In his pocket, he always carried a joiner's flat-sided pencil, a few useful pieces of string and a penknife. We enjoyed watching while he carefully cut the skin of an orange into segments and then slowly peeled them off one by one. He could sharpen our pencils with his penknife as efficiently as any pencil sharpener.

His interest in music was as lively as ever and we were accustomed to him singing around the house. It was when he whistled that our ears twitched. If we were singing he would sometimes whistle along with us. Unfortunately, it was in a different key! Despairing glances were exchanged between us. If we changed key to suit him, he unconsciously changed his. We could never win. We never told him for fear of hurting his feelings and we learned to live with it.

In the early thirties, Dad bought a motorbike with a vast sidecar. On Saturday and Sunday afternoons in summer, he packed Mother into the sidecar with Jean on her knee, Betty in front with me, and Jim on the pillion. Then we all waited while he got into the required gear of yellow waterproof coat and goggles. Then we were off to Longniddry or Gullane. The roads were quiet and our speed was never over thirty miles an hour. We felt perfectly safe. Mother enjoyed these outings as much as we did and what a joy it must have been for her to get away from the house for a while.

Mother was the other rock of security in our lives. She was always there when we came in from school or work. We gave her a shout as soon as we came through the front door and an answering call invariably came from the kitchen. Often she poured oil on the troubled waters of family relationships. She never criticised our friends and never tried to influence any of us in our choice of life partners. Along with the women of her generation, Mother took life seriously, conscious of having the responsibility of encouraging in her children the high standards in conduct which she considered to be essential for a happy and successful life. In spite of that, she had a great sense of humour. Many a laugh we had in her company. She could always see the funny side of a situation. My father was not so free and easy.

Respectable ladies of Mother's generation never wore makeup. Only actresses did that and only then on stage — never in the street. Mother had been an exceptionally attractive young girl and although her short hair was iron grey now, she still had her expressive eyes inherited from her mother and her slim upright figure. Her attitude to clothes and fashion was rather conservative. She was always neatly dressed in sober styles and colours, without fussy frills as befitted a mother of eight children. When she was going somewhere special, she heated her curling tongs on the gas cooker and crimped her hair in front of the mirror. That was her only concession to dressing up. She wore no face powder, rouge, or lipstick. Once in my teens I chummed her to the Store to buy a hat and persuaded her to buy a lovely straw one with hearts and flowers on it. It was the kind of hat I was too young to wear. She looked sensational in it but after a few outings we never saw it again. She probably considered she was past all that vanity.

My mother was the proud possessor of a fur coat. That has a story attached to it which is worth telling. Dad was a great joiner, but was no financial wizard. You see, he had this strange idea that everyone was as honest as himself. He was often disappointed when customers left large accounts outstanding even after many reminders. One firm in particular whose shop he had fitted out, delayed paying their sizeable account. Mother, who was made of sterner stuff, persuaded him to visit the firm, who were furriers to trade, and offered to go with him. So off the two of them went, not knowing what kind of reception they would get. When they returned, Mother said to the assembled family "we have a new member of the family". This was received with "modified rapture", in W.S. Gilbert's words! They all went through the possibilities. What could it be? Another child? There were enough of those already. A cat? A dog? No. It was a fur coat with which the furriers cleared their debt. My father would rather have had the money, but it was a lovely coat. It lasted for many years. I borrowed it myself when I was about twenty years old.

Ever since Mother's serious illness, we had helped with the housework. Friday evenings were given to catching up with weekly rather than daily chores. No "dates" with boyfriends were made for that evening. The kitchen and scullery floors were thoroughly scrubbed and polished. The cutlery was cleaned using a knifeboard for the knives. The parlour carpet, the runner in the lobby and on the stair were brushed with a stiff brush. Eventually, Dad bought a Hoover to make the work easier. Any brass work was "Brassoed" so you could see your face in it. The doormat and fireside rugs were taken down to the green and thoroughly thrashed to get the grit out.

The three kids, at first too young to be trusted with housework, played their part by doing the shopping on Saturday mornings. Sometimes when it was my turn, by the time I set out for my shopping expedition, I had already been down to Portobello Baths for a swim. My hair was still dripping wet when I left the house to get the messages Mother needed. In winter, that was living dangerously!

On Mondays, the washerwoman came to do the washing and hang it out to dry. The older girls took turns with the ironing after their work in the evenings. Mother managed to cope with the cooking of the midday dinner, although sometimes the girls made the main meal for the next day on the previous evening which meant Mother had only to heat it up. We made our own tea if Mother was ill.

Our cooking experiments were not always successful. Jean once made rather unusual lentil soup. Mother gave her instructions from her bed. "Remember to put a pinch of baking soda in the soup," she said. By mistake, Jean added washing soda instead. Dad ate his soup without comment and seemed not to notice anything wrong. You would think it would have discoloured the spoon, or even bent it! It was by dint of mistakes like these that we became competent housewives later.

When summer came, life was easier for Mother. She was up and about and appeared to be her old self again but when winter came, she was often in bed for part of each day. She wanted so desperately to be well that she was always following some cranky diet. One disgusting remedy was to drink the water in which cabbage had been boiled. Fortunately, she did not expect us to join in. The smell was enough for us! My father did everything he could to help her, and Spence the Chemist must have made a fortune selling him Iron Jelloids, Wincarnis Wine, Virol, and Scott's Emulsion.

On the whole, we were a fairly healthy lot. It was considered to be a good thing if, by the time you started school, you had had measles, chicken pox, and whooping cough, otherwise you would acquire them there. Considering we were such a big family, we had very few illnesses among us and in spite of the older ones rattling around on the pillions of motorbikes, roller skating and hill walking, they never had broken limbs. However, Jim achieved that distinction when he was eleven years old. While kicking a ball around with his chums, he fell awkwardly and broke his arm. Our doctor drove him to hospital to have it set. That night he was quite ill and had a sleepless night. The next day he had to be taken back to hospital to have the arm re-broken and re-set. Betty had to take him to the outpatients department for a while until the plaster was removed, as Mother was not well enough to accompany him. Jim used to strengthen his arm by exercising it on our lilac tree, the only tree we had in our garden.

We were not often absent from school or work. If we got up in the morning moaning about how awful we felt, we were told to get washed and dressed and see how we felt then. Nine times out of ten, we went off to school or work and by dinner time we had forgotten that we had begun the day feeling poorly.

Dad had an occasional bout of 'flu in the winter. When he did, the whole household had to know about it. The word went round "Dad's got 'flu. He'll be dying I expect", was the usual comment. We all knew he was on the mend when he asked one of us to go for a fish supper from the chip shop. He would eat the lot and then ask for a drink of water. Having knocked that back, he would then declare "the best thing about eating chips is the drink of water afterwards!" We knew then he would be out at work the next day!

My parents had their own remedies for illnesses not serious enough to call in our doctor. Dad's cure for an upset stomach was either a Seidlitz Powder in water, or enough of Dr Gregory's Mixture to go on an old thrupenny bit mixed with water. Since that awful tasting powder refused to dissolve in water, however much we shook it up, we swallowed it as fast as we could. You could taste it for hours afterwards, but I have to admit it did the trick!

For constipation, Mother swore by California Syrup of Figs, advertised as "nature's own laxative". It was quite pleasant tasting and very effective. For diarrhoea, we were given endless drinks of hot milky liquids. Another remedy given us in spring to "purefy the blood" was sulphur and black treacle mixed together. A teaspoonful of that gave you food for thought, especially if you happened to strike an unabsorbed pocket of sulphur. Your social life suffered too because of the resultant farts when it finally worked its way down into your system.

For cuts and bruises, unless they needed stitches, Dad sloshed hydrogen peroxide over them and bound them up. Then he kept a daily check on them in case you got the dreaded blood poisoning. He was an amateur dentist too at times. When Jean came back from hospital after having scarlet fever and her adenoids out, she had a baby tooth sticking straight out over the permanent one. Dad had the remedy. A thread was tied round the tooth and at a signal from Mother, he yanked on the thread which pulled the tooth out. Jean howled with astonishment rather than pain.

Mother's remedy for a "hoast", that is a chesty cough, was to rub camphorated oil on our chests. If we had a runny cold we were sent to bed at night with a hot lemon drink. Its preparation was all part of the ritual, as Mother always put the lemon in front of our coal fire to make the juice run freely. She probably muttered a few incantations over it as well. If we complained of a sore throat, we were made to sit over a jug of a steaming Friar's Balsam concoction, with a towel over our head so that none of the steam escaped. We had to breathe the vapours in as deeply as we could. Another sore throat cure was to take one of Dad's socks which he had worn that day, fill it with salt heated on a shovel on the open fire, then secure it round the neck at bedtime. If we had a stuffed up nose, we were over the jug again. This time a brew of mentholated crystals. Earache was treated with a little piece of cotton wool dipped in warm almond oil and placed inside the ear.

Although they trusted all these home remedies, my parents were experienced and sensible enough to know when a doctor was needed. My father paid into a family health insurance scheme, so there was no need to worry about the cost but it would never have occurred to them to call out a doctor for trivial matters. As for dental treatment, we were examined regularly by the school dentist. Our parents were informed what treatment was needed. Then we were taken to our own dentist for the treatment to be carried out.

Mother liked us to be warmly clad in winter. After the older girls went out to work, she rather lost control of what they wore and often "tut-tutted" over the thin vests, French knickers and sheer stockings they liked to wear. She herself wore a "spencer" under her dress. This was a short, lacy, fine Shetland wool garment, waist length, with elbow length sleeves. She sometimes wore knitted wrist and knee warmers too.

While she still had control of us, Jean and I were well happed up in winter. A sleeveless vest went on first, then a fleecy lined Liberty Bodice, warm knickers elasticated at waist and thigh, long black stockings and black lacing shoes. We often wore a kilt with a white cotton bodice and a woollen jersey on top. A warm scarf went round the neck, crossed over the chest and safety pinned at the back. We always had navy blue "nap" coats, made from woollen material with the nap brushed up. When it was very cold, we wore fleecy lined gaiters buttoned with a button hook up the side of the leg to the knee. A pair of woollen gloves kept our hands warm.

Our older sisters had a fairly free hand to dress as they liked. They did their best to keep up with the latest fashions, as far as their budget would allow. They loved to go dancing although they never took dancing lessons. Ballroom dancing just seemed to come naturally to them. They enjoyed a night at the pictures, and sitting talking and smoking in cafés. The rules about smoking were tested by Netta. My father smoked cigarettes but the news that his daughters smoked had not yet been broken to him. They were sitting round the fire one Sunday afternoon and Netta, the brazen hussy, took out a packet of fags, and offered them around. Mother looked fearfully at Dad, expecting an explosion. She said, "Dad, have these girls to be allowed to smoke?" Dad, lowering his Sunday paper, looked over his specs at them and said, "So long as they don't smoke mine!" So that was the subject settled. We all gave up smoking later in our lives. So did he.

What cultural changes my parents had seen since they first started out together. No one bothered any more if children played in the streets, or if washing was hung out, or jazz was played on a piano or the radio on a Sunday. It had become acceptable for women to smoke in public, although not in the street. One or two of us were caught doing that and got a severe talking to by Dad. Women wore shorts or trousers and painted their faces and fingernails; they went on the pillions of motorcycles, danced with young men they knew nothing about, went hiking and cycling and generally conducted themselves in an unseemly fashion. As they surveyed their family of five young adults and three schoolchildren, they certainly thought, and frequently said, "what's the world coming to!"

CHAPTER 13

Salad days

I started at Leith Academy Secondary School in 1932 when it was a new and much admired building. I had to work much harder there than at Hermy to keep a good place in class. Two of the subjects I hated from the start. My memory is kind to me and I cannot even remember what marks I got or even the teachers' names. These two subjects were mathematics and science. My brain seized up like an engine lacking oil as soon as I entered those classrooms. I loathed the smell of the laboratories. I saw no point in callings things 'x', 'y' and 'z', or studying triangles. In my whole life in various jobs and bringing up a family, I have still to find a use for them. In Latin, French, English, history, geography, art and music, I did quite well.

The teachers, as at primary school, were firm but fair. There was a very large lady who taught art on the top floor and a lovely lady who taught us music. When I say "she taught us music", I mean she played the piano while we sang, and pressed us to sing in school choirs. If we wanted to learn to read music we had to go to a private music teacher.

The lady who coached us in Bible study was not very good at controlling classes so I am ashamed to say we gave her a hard time every week. All our teachers were Misses. Every Miss who became Mrs had to leave to make way for another Miss.

Our English teacher was a small older man with white hair and a trim white moustache. He whirled into the classroom, his gown billowing out behind him and commanded instant quiet and attention before he started his lesson. If you failed to learn anything in his class, you were hopeless. He was very sharp and could spot a slacker a mile away.

History was one of my favourite subjects. The man who taught us had been injured in the war. He treated his subject seriously and somehow his lesson stuck in your mind. Whoever taught me geography has faded from my memory but I always managed to get through the exams without too much trouble.

The lady who taught us French had a strange habit of calling me "Frances". At first I looked around to see if we had a Frances in the class. Then it dawned on me she was looking directly at me. Several times I had to tell her my name was not Frances. Each time she would say "Oh, yes, you're Nancy Harris. I keep calling you Frances because I once had a Frances Harris in a class." She never did come to terms with my name, so I gave in and became Frances in her class and Nancy everywhere else.

It was difficult to see any future use for Latin, an apparently dead language, but the smattering I gained helps a great deal in guessing the meaning of words when a dictionary is not available.

The teacher who put us through our paces in physical education was a remarkable lady. Not young, but a proper dynamo of energy, slim, wiry and powerful. She had no patience with slackers. If some hapless girl came with a note from her mother to "please excuse so-and-so as she is unwell this week", a euphemism for menstruating, she gave the girl a withering look guaranteed to reduce her to an embarrassed jelly and concentrated on the rest of us.

One of the highlights of the school year was the school concert which took place before we broke up for the summer holidays. I was always in a choir of some sort, and there were talented people who could sing solo or recite. There were usually a few funny sketches with thinly veiled impersonations of our teachers, which they took in good part. The school orchestra did its best to massacre a bit of Mozart or Bach. For such a special occasion, the teachers wore their mortar boards, as well as their gowns and stoles. Very impressive they looked. We, of course, wore our school uniforms of shapeless pleated gymslip buttoned at the shoulder, dragged in at the waist with a fringed tie belt and white blouse.

Another big day was the sports day held at Hawkhill. If the weather was good everyone enjoyed it. By this time I had lost my enthusiasm for running but we all went just the same if only to spot the talent and chat up the boys!

Apart from school and work, the Harrises were great joiners of organisations and took part in leisure activities with enthusiasm.

In spite of the enforced marriage with Edinburgh, Leith kept its separate flavour. The place fairly hummed with life and opportunities for young people to enjoy. Brownies, Guides and Scouts were all part of the same movement and as well as weekly meetings, there were camps in summer, concerts to practice for, country dancing, picnics and outings. On our picnics we cooked sausages and eggs over an open fire. In theory, the eggs were pierced and if they survived that without breaking, we put them near the heat to cook. That was usually the end of them! The sausages always ended up with a hard burned overcoat. We were always desperately hungry, so unless they actually caught fire, we ate them.

One Guide camp I went to near West Linton remains in memory for various reasons. There was never enough hot water to wash our mountains of greasy dishes. The weather was not very good either. But worst of all, the midges took a fancy to me. When my face blew up like a balloon and my eyes disappeared, those in authority decided it was time to take action. They took me to a local doctor who prescribed painting my face with calamine lotion. I looked a sight. When my mother saw me she nearly had a fit.

At the Guides' Hallow'een party, we ate mashed potatoes and turnip, dooked for apples, cracked nuts with our teeth and tried to catch treacle scones. The scones, generously slaggered with black treacle, were suspended from a string and with our hands tied behind our backs, we were expected to catch one in our mouths! I always did my best to avoid involvement in that!

On the serious side, we learned about tying knots, first aid, signalling with Morse code and with flags, and many other things, some useful, some not.

We joined choirs, not necessarily attached to our own church. I recall being in a children's choir at Claremont Church at the foot of Easter Road. The choir master was very good with young people and produced a Kinderspiel which was a strong attraction. We loved dressing up and what we lacked in talent, we made up for in enthusiasm.

The rewards for our loyalty to the organisations we attended were well worth the trouble. The Sunday School trips each summer were much anticipated events. When the chosen Saturday came round, we assembled at the church hall with our "tinnies" slung round our necks on a tape, and our tea tickets safely in our pockets. We formed up in twos and walked to the tram or bus stop. We never went very far on these occasions although it seemed far to us. Favourite places were Currie, Balerno, Juniper Green and Granton. Each class was in the charge of their teacher. They were our mothers for that day. One I remember very well. When she was not a Sunday School teacher, she worked for an Edinburgh publisher. She always organised a few races just for her own class with lovely book prizes. There were other games and races to take up the afternoon until the time for tea arrived. Then we sat down on the grass in rows, while helpers poured strong tea into our "tinnies". In return for our tea ticket, we got a paper bag containing a tuppenny pie, a scone, a cake and some biscuits each. It was a feast.

It was understood that if it rained, we would have the picnic in the hall but I cannot recall a single time when that happened. I should say this does not mean we never had rain. It means we put up with it rather than have the picnic in the church hall.

Around five o'clock, the teachers rounded us up and we made our way in an orderly fashion to the nearest tram or bus stop. Once back at the hall, we only had to walk through the Links and up Lochened Road and we were home.

The high point in the year for most organisations was the Christmas party. All the girls dressd up in their party dresses and the boys in their best shorts and shirts with slicked back hair. Jean and I were very lucky as our sister Madeline made our dresses, both exactly the same. I remember one year she made lovely pale pink dresses with layers of petals for the skirt.

We played all the old fashioned games such as "Musical Chairs", or "Musical Arms", "Pass the parcel", "Here's a poor widow who's left alone", "The farmer's in the dell", and the "Grand old Duke of York". At one such party I received my first proposal of marriage. My suitor was all of eleven years old. He went around telling everyone he was going to marry me, much to the amusement of the grownups, and to my mortification! After all, I hadn't said "yes". I spent most of the time at that party dodging him, nearly dead with embarrassment. Thankfully, I never saw him again!

My father was a Mason and we considered their party to be the best. They really knew how to entertain us and our expectations of a good time were never disappointed. There was a big Christmas tree on the platform at one end of the hall, with tables laden with gifts. We knew that Santa Clause would come whether we believed in him or not and that each child would receive a present. We had games, sandwiches, icecream, and lemonade, in fact, as much as we could take. Some of the men dressed up as clowns or golliwogs, and each one would take a group of children into a corner of the hall and play guessing games or have a singsong. Then the announcement was made that Santa Claus was coming. The lights dimmed. We lined up in two long lines on either side of the big fireplace. Then up went the lights! With his sack over his shoulder, he ran the gauntlet of clapping, cheering, children to where the gifts were laid out and he then began handing one to each child. They were always good quality gifts and we appreciated them very much.

Guide Christmas parties were sometimes fancy dress affairs, and most ingenious the outfits were, often made from things begged or borrowed from members of the family. Jean once made good use of a leather coat belonging to Netta. It had cost her £8 but she was tired of it. Jean made a fringed skirt from it and borrowed Jim's Scout hat to complete her outfit as a cowgirl. Another time, she hired a Spanish costume paid for with money she saved up for a few weeks.

Entertainment was plentiful in Leith. Apart from going to the pictures, there were always Guide and Scout concerts, amateur concert parties and drama groups. There were professional shows at the Gaiety and the Studio Theatre. Home-made entertainment was not lacking, and Jean and her chums used to arrange concerts. Family and friends were dragooned into attending, to suffer and applaud. We often had sing-songs on a Sunday evening, sitting round the kitchen fire. Sometimes we were joined by one or two "outsiders", perhaps a school friend of one of us. As the girls grew older, a boyfriend or two joined us as well. These visitors were accepted without fuss by our parents and no embarrassing remarks were made about the relationship. There was a lot of coming and going when the older girls were at the courting stage but there was never any comment when one boyfriend got the elbow and another took his place. It was usually we young ones who were disappointed when a boyfriend got the heave, especially if he had been generous to us in the hope that he could worm his way into our sister's affection through us.

The greatest contribution to the entertainment of the three kids came when Dad got rid of the old motor cycle combination, and bought a car instead. It was an Arrol-Johnston, second-hand, made in Paisley, big as a house, and already a car which commanded the kind of awe attracted by vintage cars today. He bought it from a Leith businessman. No driving test was needed in those days. A driving lesson, the only one my father ever had, was given free by the seller. It consisted of a run along Salamander Street and back! When new, the car was advertised thus:-

---

Arrol-Johnston

Cars offer you a WIDER RADIUS OF COUNTRY.
Neither hills nor bad roads affect their
clockwork regularity of speed.

"Many week-ends my Arrol-Johnston does
300 to 400 miles (Saturday to Sunday evening)
— extremely comfortable and steady —
no hills in Scotland too steep to stop her —
have not had to touch her."

(Signed) W.W. Hill,
The Links,
Peterhead.

Arrol-Johnston Ltd.
PAISLEY

People used to come up to us while Dad cranked the handle to start it and say in hushed tones, as though speaking of the dead, "Is this an Arrol-Johnston?" We modestly said "yes", and basked in the admiration of the enquirers while they toured round the car examining it from all angles and caressing it reverently.

Our car opened up an area of entertainment we barely knew existed. Every Saturday and Sunday in the summer, we went to some of our favourite places taking a picnic tea, and sometimes dinner as well. Dad made a special "tuck box", which was like a small coffin divided into compartments, to accommodate a few sticks to start a fire, the kettle, the Primus stove, the sandwiches and other food, and the dishes and cutlery.

Sometimes on a Sunday we made a whole day of it. We took care to leave at a time when church goers were unlikely to see us, in case it could be thought we were enjoying ourselves! My father garaged the car at his workshop in James' Lane so he had to go to collect it and bring it up to the end of our terrace. On a fine Sunday morning, Mother shouted up the stairs to those of us still in bed, "Dad's away for the car". We had it timed to the last second how much longer we had in bed before leaping out to get dressed. Mother prepared sandwiches, hard boiled eggs, and peeled potatoes, to go with the corned beef or boiled ham, for Dad to put in the tuckbox. Sometimes, we were allowed to take a friend, if there was room in the car. Then as soon as the car was loaded, we were off.

Longniddry foreshore was a favourite place of ours. We made out little camp on the grass, spreading the travelling rugs in the most sheltered place for Mother to sit. Then we flung off our clothes as quickly as possible to put on our shapeless woollen bathing costumes, and dashed into the sea with shouts of "come on in", "no, it's too cold", "you're a big coward". The older ones did not often come on these expeditions, as they were usually busy seeing their friends, but sometimes some of them arrived later on the pillions of motor cycles.

While sitting in our chosen picnic spot at Longniddry, a figure we all recognised appeared in the distance, pushing his bicycle over the uneven ground from group to group. He wore a dark uniform, cycle clips, and a cap trimmed with red. He carried a ticket machine and a bag for money. His face was dark mahogany from being out in all weathers, and he knew us as old customers. He always exchanged a few friendly words with Dad and handed over a wee ticket in return for the thrupenny bit Dad fished out of his pocket. This fee went into the coffers of the Earl of Wemyss who owned the foreshore.

We always had a "shivery bite" after being in the sea. Sometimes it was half a roll and butter and we stood eating it, goose-pimpled and blue all over, while Mother rubbed us down with a towel. Before going home, we collected buckies in the tea kettle. We took care not to take the pink buckies as we were told they were bad for us. In the early evening, we packed everything up and took our leisurely way home before lighting-up time. Dad did not enjoy driving after dark so he always consulted the daily paper to find out the lighting-up time. Once home the car was unpacked and Dad returned it to its home in his workshop. Meanwhile, we boiled up the buckies and ate them, picking them from their shells with a pin.

One day we were on our way home after such an outing. We kids were in the back, heads down, reading as usual. Suddenly, we felt a thump — our car had been hit amidships by another. I think it was one of those occasions where each driver thought the other would give way at a crossing. My mother had a bad gash on her leg and we were all a bit shaken, but apart from that, no one was badly hurt. It must have been one of the slowest accidents ever, as neither car was doing more than 5 miles an hour!

Another favourite beach was Gullane, where there was a huge grassy sheltered basin to protect us from the wind and sand dunes running straight down into the sea. When I saw Gullane again after the war, I was puzzled that it looked so unfamiliar. No grassy basin, not many dunes, what had happened to it? When I asked local people, they said the Army had used it as a training ground, completely changing its appearance. Since then, the local Council has been restoring the beach by planting marram grass.

If we were not at a seaside place, we were at the Eildon Hills, the Grey Mare's Tail, Lochearnhead, the Braes of Balquidder or Loch Lubnaig. There we paddled in the burn or the loch, kicked a ball about on the grass, climbed the lower slopes of the hills, and brought back armfuls of heather when it was in bloom.

When the traditional Spring holiday came round, if the weather was suitable, we had a big blanket washing in the morning. We took it in turns to tramp them with our feet and work up a good "graith". Then we rinsed them thoroughly and put them through the wringer. When we took them down to the green, two of us took two corners each and flicked the blankets up and down vigorously, to shake off any excess water and fluff. After that, they were hung up on ropes to dry. In the afternoon, we each followed our own preferences. My older sisters liked to walk in the Pentland Hills, and we young ones joined our chums to play strenuous games in the terrace or in the Links.

In the evening, the older girls, who probably had "dates" with boyfriends, went off to the pictures or to the dancing. We younger ones played kick-the-can at the end of the terrace, or rounders, skipping ropes, or tig.

The Autumn holiday was spent in much the same way, catching up with the housework in the mornings and going out and about in the afternoon and evening. We were given a great deal of freedom. If we were up to something we thought our parents would disapprove of, we very kindly shielded them from the knowledge!

A benefit which came to us as my father's business prospered, was a yearly holiday. He and Charlie still only had the Trades Week and that unpaid, but the rest of us had a whole fortnight away from home. We went camping several times, and on one memorable occasion we were nearly washed away. Mother was in charge, as Dad and Charlie were both working that week. When the rain, thunder and lightning started, Mother found it quite exciting standing at the flap of the tent with Betty, the rain stotting on her umbrella, watching the lightning bounce over the hills. Jean and I were fast asleep and oblivious to the situation. Jim was awake enjoying the excitement. But soon the thrill of the storm was replaced by alarm as it became clear we might be washed into the river. My poor mother must have been worried to death. We were expecting Charlie to arrive from Leith that Friday night so she waited, not knowing how to cope with the situation. Then she heard the welcome sound of Charlie's motorbike. He organised the adults to dig a trench round our bell tent but it was no use. The rain continued to pelt down and the river threatened to engulf us, so Charlie went for help to a railwayman's bothy not far away. These surfacemen, bless their hearts, came to our rescue. Jean and I were carried to their bothy where there was a roaring fire in front of which we all slept comfortably for the rest of that night! What an adventure to talk about when we got home! I have no memory of how we dried everything out and made our soggy way back to Sunny Leith.

I have to admit that we hardly ever had unbroken sunny weather, and it was often cold and wet, but we were always determined to enjoy ourselves come what may!

It was about this time when things were going so well for my father that he branched out into the building trade. He took on more employees and sub-contracted to other trades. He built three bungalows on the south side of Milton Road. At that time they were quite expensive, at £960 for a semi-detached one, and £1,050 for a detached one. Later he built several terraced houses in Summerfield Gardens at around £750. They were of much better quality than the inferior lower priced houses which were being thrown up in schemes around Edinburgh in the thirties. He worked longer and harder than any of his men. Often on a Sunday, Betty, Jean and I walked up to the Milton Road houses through Restalrig Village, to take him sandwiches and a flask of tea for his midday meal. He was now at the head of a sizeable workforce.

With my father so busy, it was left to Mother to cope with family matters. Her health had not deteriorated so much as to affect that. Of course, the girls had evolved a routine of household help for her which made it possible for her to carry on — but she did have to conserve her energies. We knew not to expect her at parents' days at school, or sports days, or anything which needed stamina. She just did not have it.

In the Pirniefield corner of Leith, Granny Brown still lived in Seafield Avenue. She was in her seventies now, and still quite active. She and the son and daughter from her second marriage, and their families, were the only relatives we had left in that area which had teemed with Harrises and Rutherfords such a short time ago.

Over the years, my mother kept in touch with her sister, our Auntie Mary. She sometimes came to visit us for a few days, bringing her only son with her. She, like my mother, had kept her good looks and slender figure, and her sense of humour was undiminished.

Uncle Johnny and Auntie Jean who had been such benefactors to us when my parents were less well off, came back to Edinburgh to live so that their two sons could complete their education. We visited them from time to time in the large house they had in Murrayfield. As always, we were impressed by their lifestyle but not particularly envious.

My father's sister, Auntie Annie, who had deserted Scotland when she married, came to see us too, but in general, there was not a great deal of communication between these surviving members of the two families who had once been so close. My parents were not the kind who went out paying calls and with so many people in our home, there was no room for entertaining visitors.

Uncle Will, my father's brother, still lived in Leith. Will's health had not improved and life could not have been easy for him. For a time he was a warder in Saughton Prison, and we were taken to visit the family there once. That occasion must have made a strong impression on our Jim. Returning from a Sunday School trip in a loaded bus which passed the prison, he announced to one and all " my uncle's in there". He had some explaining to do to his shocked teacher!

Will's family lived in Dalmeny Street eventually and it was there at the age of 45 that his slender hold on life gave way and he died in January 1933. It was Granny Brown who came to tell us of Will's death. The old lady appeared at our kitchen door and abruptly announced "Wull's deid".

She did not survive Will for long. She died peacefully in her sleep in May 1934. The family found her in bed, hands neatly clasped on her breast. She was seventy-four years old. Her early life had been far from happy, but she had lived long enough to see her large family prosper and leave poverty behind them.

In spite of these sad events, the thirties were full of interesting and happy occasions as well. It was inevitable that courtship and marriage should become an important part of our lives with so many eligible young people in our house. We had a positive epidemic of love and marriage. Five weddings between 1934 and 1938! Charlie was the first to find romance and for the next twenty odd years, romances, marriages and births abounded in our family.

CHAPTER 14

Love and marriage

From our lowly station in life as the three kids, we had an ideal opportunity to observe our elder brother and four sisters as they each reached maturity. Jean and I gained a great deal of enjoyment from listening to the girls' conversations in our bedroom. Romance and all that stuff seemed very far ahead of us so their talk of this or that boy, whether he was fat or skinny, tall or short, blue eyed or brown eyed, pimply or not, gave us great amusement. They thought we were fast asleep so we had to stifle our giggles under the bedclothes!

Our Charlie managed to get along in this houseful of women by keeping quiet. He had his own little room and when he returned from work and had had tea, he disappeared into his room to read. He was always good natured and never joined in the frequent squabbles of his sisters. He was more of a thinker than a talker. Often he was teased by the girls about being an "absent minded professor". This was with good reason. On one occasion he cycled down to the workshop with a coat hanger still in his jacket, looking like the hunchback of Notre Dame. Another time he went off with two caps on his head. He took the jokes in good part.

He was a real sleepy head in the mornings, probably because he had been reading half the night. Dad called him again and again to get him to work. Charlie was aware of the problem himself and even fitted up a contraption so that his alarm clock rang far enough away so that he had to get up to shut if off. He had a very dry and pawky sense of humour but as he was twelve years older than me, this escaped my notice until we were both a lot older.

There was a whole lot more to Charlie than met the eye, and for all his apparent shyness, romance found him without having to look too hard. He met Cathie at Dickson's Dancing Classes in Albany Street. She was with a girlfriend and he was with a male friend, so they made a foursome of it for a week or so, changing partners for the various dances. One night, the other two were absent for some reason from the regular class, so Charlie saw Cathie home. After that, they started going out together. They had had only three dates when he took her on the back of his motorbike to Gullane beach, intending to propose to her. It was a beautiful evening and the sand stretched away into the distance unmarked by human feet. It should have been a most romantic occasion, but unfortunately, Charlie sat on the hooter button of the motorbike. They laughed so much that the romantic moment was gone, so there was no proposal that night. Finally, he proposed on a bench on the Calton Hill, after they had been to the Playhouse Cinema nearby. Cathie said "yes" and he brought her home to meet us. It must have been quite a shock for her as her family was not as big as ours. Cathie was a good pianist and elocutionist, and we three children were always pestering her to play or recite to us. Very often she obliged.

They announced their engagement at Mamie's twenty-first birthday party in March 1933 and married in January 1934. It was a white wedding. The minister performed the ceremony in the presence of all the guests in the hall in which the reception took place. Jim got his first set of "longs" for the occasion, and Jean and I had new dresses. It could have been taken as a bad omen when Charlie's suit for the wedding arrived from the tailor's with a label which read "Urgent for funeral"! On the contrary, it has been the cause of laughter ever since.

My father's present to the young couple was a very practical one. He gave them as much timber as they needed from his workshop to build cupboards or anything else they required.

In the twenty-six years since my parents married, fashions in weddings had changed a lot. Then, the marriage often took place in the bride's parents' home. In the inter-war years, there were several choices. It could be in the bride's church, or in the vestry of the church, or the Manse, or a local hall hired for the reception, or the Registry Office. The last mentioned was considered to be not quite respectable, implying a need for haste and secrecy. A Gretna Green wedding also indicated haste but was considered to be very romantic! That took rather more courage than any of us had! Mother and Dad would have been horrified!

It was accepted that young couples did not rush into marriage. Engagements could last quite a long time while both parties saved up to start a home together. In our family, all the first five were into their twenties when they married, and had quite long courtships and engagements.

After Charlie's marriage, Netta was the next one to take the plunge. She had been Dad's clerkess for about ten years by then. She had taken a six months business course at Skerry's College in preparation for her job. Her wage when she started was 10/- (50 pence) a week. She gave 9/- (45 pence) to Mother. This may seem a lot but for that she got all her food and clothes. Then as her wage increased over the years, she gradually took over her own finances. This was the system followed by the rest of us in our turn.

She attended nightschool at Leith Academy a couple of evenings a week. Most young people did that to improve their skills with a view to "bettering themselves". It was also part of the social life of the young where they met their friends and members of the opposite sex. After nightschool, the students usually adjourned to a local café for coffee and conversation.

In her spare time, Netta played golf, often with my father before they started work in the morning. As he started at 8 am they had to be out very early. She liked to walk in the Pentlands, and often went to motor cycle meetings, picnics and dances. Although she had had no formal training, she was very good at making her own clothes. Even some of her hats were created at home.

She met her future husband on Portobello promenade while walking with a girlfriend. He was walking with a friend of his and as the two friends knew each other, there were soon introductions all round. From there the romance blossomed. They were married in the drawing room of St John's manse and we had a small reception at home. We were finding bits of hard white bridal icing in odd corners for weeks afterwards!

Our family was dwindling and there were signs of other defectors too. During these years of courtship and marriage there was a constant stream of suitors to our house. The girls were all attractive and lively. They loved parties. Our Mamie was given the choice of a party or a wristwatch for her twenty-first birthday. She naturally chose a party. The girls did all the food preparation themselves. The rule was soft drinks only but perhaps some of the young lads had an alcoholic drink before they arrived. They played parlour games such as Postman's Knock, Forfeits, Kissing all the flowers on the carpet, Musical chairs, or arms, Putting the tail on the donkey. Sometimes there was a quiz with a bar of chocolate for the winner. A lot of these games gave opportunities for kissing members of the opposite sex. Some couples found a haven on our inside stair for a bit of petting but there were no orgies. We young ones were allowed to join in or watch the games and it was all very innocent. My mother and father stayed in the kitchen keeping an ear open for any over-boisterous behaviour.

One New Year we had a lovely party. All the paper chains and paper bells which lived in the parlour cupboard the rest of the year were hung up. There was the usual festive fare, black bun, Christmas cake and shortbread. The girls made sandwiches, jelly, trifle and fairy cakes. There was lemonade, Kola and American Cream Soda to drink. As usual, Mother and Dad sat by the kitchen fire taking no active part. Then Mother said in one of her gentle wheedling voices, "Dad, go ben and speak to the young folk". Dad reluctantly got up from his armchair and did as he was told. He opened the door of the parlour which was crammed with cheerful young men and girls. There was silence as he appeared. Some of the young men shuffled their feet and mumbled "Hello, Mr Harris". As head of the household, he expected, and got, their respectful attention. He looked slowly around him and then delivered the immortal words "fine cannon fodder for the next war". Those words came back to haunt us later as, within a few years, these young men were fighting and dying in the Second World War.

In the summer of 1936, Madeline married. This gave my mother an opportunity to line up the whole family for a photograph once again. As she was fifty years old now, her confidence that her family was complete was at last justified. Another reason for the photograph was that Madeline was marrying an Aberdonian and leaving us to live in Aberdeen. To my mother, it might as well have been the moon. Certainly, there would be less opportunity for family reunions after that.

This sister was quiet, like Charlie. She never joined in with the other girls in their talk about boyfriends and dates. She took life seriously and had been very involved in Guides, church, Sunday

School, and choirs. Somehow she acquired a mature air very early in life. She never did any of the daft things the other girls did; she never had to be sewn into her party frock like Netta; never had funny stories to tell from her work as Mamie did; never splashed out on six-inch heeled shoes, or an Eton crop like Betty did. She made all her own clothes. As she had been trained in Patrick Thomson's workroom as a dressmaker, they were always beautiful.

She had a dressmaker's dummy called Deborah. Deborah's skin was rather greyish. She had no head, no arms, and her feet were replaced by a three-legged wooden base. To suggest she had breasts would be to overstate the case, and certainly no nipples. She stood, armless, legless, headless, and indifferent while Madeline fitted garments on her, sticking pins into her padded torso. She was kept in our bedroom and could give us quite a fright if we woke in the middle of the night and saw her figure in the dim light. We gave her a dance sometimes in our dafter moments at parties. She went to Aberdeen with Madeline.

Many nice young men were interested in Madeline but she treated them very coolly. In the end, she rejected them all to marry a man she met when she was on holiday in Aberdeen. On Sundays, he came to court her by the day excursion train from Aberdeen. The fare was 8/- (40 pence) return. It was a strange courtship, we thought. He seemed so much older than our sister, but he was her choice and my parents made no attempt to influence her.

She had a lovely white wedding. The ceremony and the reception took place in Smith's Rooms, and then our sister went off to Aberdeen to start a new life. So Jean and I lost our favourite dressmaker, and there were no more pretty party frocks. We had to buy them after that.

We three kids were in our early teens now, still standing on the sidelines of life. Jim was working out his apprenticeship with my father. He was tall and lanky, all legs and curly brown hair. The highlight of 1937 for him was the Scout Jamboree he went to in Vogelnzang in Holland. Dressed in the kilt, the Scottish contingent must have been an astonishing sight dancing in the main arena. A "thirty-twosome" was in the middle, two "sixteensomes" on either side, and about ten eightsomes round the perimeter. They marched on and off behind a pipe band playing "The Black Bear". They had a wonderful fortnight of unbroken sunshine. When he came home and told us about it, we felt as if we had been there ourselves.

Mother, Dad, Jean and I went to Dunoon for our summer holiday that year and Netta with her baby daughter came with us. We stayed in a guest house in the West Bay. My father was only there for the Trades Week. Every day we took a leisurely stroll to buy provisions for our landlady to cook for us, then we sat in the open air bandstand listening to the band, or to the records they played. There was rather a lot of "Ah, sweet mystery of life" that year, I remember. Sometimes we walked along the promenade to marvel at the man who played tunes on an ordinary saw. Often we were snapped by those highwaymen, the street photographers. They gave us a little ticket and we took it to their kiosk later in the day and had a look at the photos. If we liked them, we bought them. In the ones we brought back from Dunoon, we look relaxed and happy, with no indication of the problems my father had to face when we got back to Leith.

My father's business was in difficulties. Never very good at handling the financial side and always too lenient with his customers, his creditors would not wait for their money and he was in danger of bankruptcy. It was as much a blow to his pride as his pocket. There was a meeting of his creditors and, entirely due to the respect in which he was held by the business community, bankruptcy was avoided. Mr Yuill of Kersans undertook to straighten out everything and bought over my father's debts. He proved himself to be a true friend, as he had always been in the many years he had known my father.

When my mother broke the news of the collapse of Dad's business to us, we found it hard to believe. My father was in a very depressed state and after the creditor's meeting, he walked out of our house and was gone for several hours. Mother had no idea where he had gone and was worried about him in his state of mind. We were all thankful to see his return but he never discussed his problems with us at any time. By the time things were settled, it was plain that the workshop could carry on. Mr Yuill, that generous man, saw to it that my father had enough orders for packing boxes for the meat packing industry to keep him going. It was not easy as there were deadlines to meet. All of us helped at one time or another to stack up the pieces of wood as they came off the machine in the evenings after our own daily work. Our way of life changed very little as we were all working and bringing in our own contributions to the household finances. In the midst of this upheaval, Betty was planning to marry in November.

Betty met her future husband at a Bowling Club dance in Smith's Rooms. It was "formal", that is to say, he was in a dinner suit from the 50/- tailors, and she was wearing a long evening frock. They began going steady after that. They had quite a long courtship of three or four years before they married. I was her bridesmaid at the ceremony in the vestry of St John's. The reception was in our house with just close members of the two families.

Since I had grown up, Betty often lent me her clothes. She was a shop assistant in Patrick Thomsons and then in J. & R. Allan on the Bridges, and enjoyed her work very much. Like the rest of us, she was an enthusiastic joiner of organisations but she liked to be different too. So while the rest of us joined Guides, she chose the Girls' Guildry. It had the same aims as the Guides. Their uniform was simple. It was a plain white blouse and dark skirt with a coloured sash over the shoulder.

In her salad days, she went to Leith Academy nightschool to learn shorthand and typing. She enjoyed playing tennis on the courts in the Links, a night at the pictures, and sitting in the West End Café, as close to the band as possible so that she could "make eyes" at the band. Although she had such a confident manner, she was quite timid underneath. She was rather frightened of bicycles, but would have been the last to admit it. She never learned to swim because on one occasion she had opened her eyes underwater, and the experience put her off. She loved to be up to date with fashionable clothes; sheer silk stockings and very high heeled shoes, smart suits over flimsy underwear, were her delight. None of us had gold or silver jewellery but Betty always had some nice costume jewellery and allowed me to wear it sometimes.

When she left Edinburgh to join her husband in Southampton, I chummed her to Waverley Station. At that time in her life, everything was a last minute rush and I remember how the pair of us went galloping down the Waverley steps at breakneck speed, the suitcases bumping on every step. She caught the train by the skin of her teeth, leaving me feeling hot, rumpled, and fuming on the platform. Even then, I hated to be rushed or in danger of being late for anything. It was quite a long time before we saw Betty again and I had forgiven her by that time!

After she left the nest, Mamie, Jim, Jean and I were the only survivors. Our parents must have thought the house very quiet after the bustle they were accustomed to. We were often out too pursuing our own affairs singlemindedly, and selfishly not giving a thought to our parents' feelings.

These years were eventful for the rest of the world as well as for our family. We had seen King Edward VIII take over the throne after George V's death, and we had discussed his liaison with Mrs Simpson, the American divorcée. He was a forty-one year old bachelor with a rather unhappy face and we thought he ought to have had more sense! His abdication at the end of 1936 was the gossip of the day and for many weeks, months, and years afterwards. His brother followed him on the throne as George VI. He and his wife and two little daughters were always in the news. The coronation in May 1937 was a cause for a big celebration in Edinburgh and Leith. There was a carnival in the Links and we made the most of that. If we had no money left, we went there anyway, just to be part of the cheerful crowds milling about the place. There was a big gala night at Portobello Pool and many school and youth organisation events. I still have the New Testament given to me by St John's to commemorate that day.

As the thirties moved on, we were more and more concerned at the situation in Germany where the Nazi movement had complete control. My father and mother's generation were convinced more and more that we would be at war with Germany before long. We of the younger generation found that difficult to accept, especially as our parents had not long ago fought the "war to end all wars". If we gave it any serious thought, it was with excitement and even anticipation, which only goes to illustrate our immaturity. However, when Hitler's troops annexed Austria, we knew we had cause to be fearful. The sight in the newsreels of Hitler reviewing his troops in Vienna did nothing to soothe us.

Not long after that, there was a serious crisis when Hitler announced that he intended to move into Czechoslovakia. Neville Chamberlain, the Prime Minister, believed that a peaceful settlement could be made. So in September 1938, Britain held its breath while he tried to negotiate face-to-face with Hitler. It was a desperately anxious time.

Some time before the crisis, our Jim and his friends from the terraces at last deserted the Scouts, to join the Territorial Army. They had weekly drills at Dalmeny Street Drill Hall and a yearly camp for instruction in the art of war. Even better, they could look forward to receiving a bounty of £5! Now they were all expected to pay for these privileges! They were all called-up to prepare for war. I remember Jim and the others, none of them more than nineteen years old, standing in Lochend Road in uniform, with their kitbags beside them, waiting for transport to collect them and take them to an unknown destination. In the fearful days which followed, we found out that Jim's Regiment was stationed around Edinburgh. Jim's section was living in railway carriages in a siding at Fillyside. We used to visit him to deliver a few home comforts.

During this unsettling time, the first big world-shaking event in our young lives, we tried to keep calm and get on with our daily work. We depended on newspapers and the wireless for details about the negotiations between Hitler and Chamberlain in Germany. When at the end of of October the Prime Minister returned from Munich to report the success of his effort, we were relieved at the news that there would be no war. But the stark reality was that he had given in to Hitler's demands, and sacrificed Czechslovakia. The Nazis moved into Czechoslovakia without delay. In the House of Commons, Winston Churchill growled, "The highwayman has demanded £1 and has grudgingly taken 18/6d, and the rest on a promissory note". It was clear this was only the beginning and the next instalment would soon be due.

Now that the crisis was over, the Territorials were released immediately from their duties to put away their uniforms and return to their normal work.

In December of that crisis year, Mamie got married. She and her "intended" had met at a motorcycle club dance and they had been going steady for five years. Although she was the smallest of us, she always had lots of energy. If she was baby-sitting with us we could be sure of some fun. She sometimes pretended to faint but she could not fool me or Jean. We used to climb over her recumbent body or ignore her altogether, and she had to give up in the end.

Mamie wore her dark hair short with a thick fringe. On one occasion she was persuaded to put curlers in her hair overnight by one of the others. In the morning when she took the curlers out, she nearly died when she saw the result. I can still see her standing in front of the mirror sobbing hysterically while trying to brush the curls out with water so that she could go to work! Later she saw the funny side of it, but she never used curlers again.

In her teens she had a strong sense of the dramatic. She once ran away from home, but only as far as our coal cellar, where she waited to see if anyone missed her. Nobody did, so she soon got fed-up and went up to tea! Another time, she and her chum went to hear an evangelist who came to Leith Town Hall. They were so carried away by his eloquence that they went up to the platform to be saved, tears of emotion in their eyes. Mother and Dad, who were there too out of curiosity, could hardly believe what they saw. She wanted to become a missionary, no less. Afterwards, Mother said to Dad "how long will it last?" Mamie made a good start and took our dog walks at night without a protest, meekly washed the dishes and did the ironing. It lasted a week. After that, she went back to normal. It was too difficult to be a Christian. She could never understand how the old Christians could face up to the lions when taking out the dog was too much for her!

Our Mamie definitely had a religious bent, and attended Carrubbers Close Mission. Another mission she attended was in Jane Street. The preacher there was a real character who went up and down Jane Street ringing a handbell to call everyone to his services — he was very goodlooking. All the girls were in love with him and he would have had no trouble even without the handbell. That mission put on amateur plays and Mamie appeared on stage in "The Little Newsboy". We went to see her in it and thought she was great in her ragged clothes and large floppy "bunnet". After that, she thought she would give up religion and go on the stage!

Like Betty, she was a shop assistant. She and her fiancé had saved up for a long time for the marriage. He earned about £3 a week and she about £2. Of course, she had to leave her work as soon as she married, so the two of them would have to live on one wage. But they could afford to rent a house and their savings helped to furnish it. The shops were now encouraging people to buy on the "never-never" system. It was "Easier to pay the 4-year way", as they advertised it. For a first instalment of 20/- (£1), you could have £48 worth of furniture to be paid up weekly. You might think that for £48 you would get very little, but you would be wrong. You could have a dining room suite of sideboard table and 4 chairs for 9 guineas (£9.45p), a Chesterfield suite for 16½ guineas (£17.32p), an easy chair for 39/6d (£2), a bed for 59/6d (£3), and a bedroom suite for 13½ guineas (£14.18p). There were no queues at the door clamouring to buy them. In fact, they had to offer inducements in the form of a free clock or something similar. Wages were very low and it was a struggle for young people to set up a home. Bed and table linen were often given in presents and it was traditional for the best maid to give a good set of china. The young couple certainly considered themselves to be among the lucky ones when they married.

The marriage took place in the vestry at St John's. All our brides had to walk the length of our terrace, under the gaze of the neighbours, to the taxi waiting to take them to the vestry or the manse. My father always observed the tradition of the "poor oot". He threw a handful of coins out of the taxi window for the children to scramble for. If there was no "poor oot", the local kids shouted "hard up" after you!

These exciting years of love and marriage made up the most formative time in the lives of the three kids. After our older sisters and brother left home, the house seemed very empty. Jim now had Charlie's old room. The big bedroom upstairs seemed even bigger to Jean and me. We even had a choice of beds now. But within a year, all our lives were changed suddenly and dramatically when the Second World War broke out.

Mamie (24), Netta (26), Jim (17), Betty (21), Madeline (23), Mother (50), Jean (13), Charlie (27), Nancy (15), Father (51)

CHAPTER 15

Fashion, food and fun

Jean and I had seen our sisters grow into womanhood, marry and leave home. We had listened to them discussing fashions in clothes and we followed their example. In a way, we profited from their mistakes. Not that we were experts by any means. We made our own mistakes.

The fashions of the thirties were very pretty, with fitted waists, draped bodices, sweetheart necklines, puffed sleeves, flattering pleated skirts a bit below the knee, court shoes in winter and "peeptoe" sandals in summer. The materials we used were linen or cotton in summer. In winter, tweed or wool, in its various forms, were used. It could be knitted or woven, or bouclé, which had a kind of knotty effect, Shetland, Angora and various weights of wool, from very fine for dresses and skirts, to heavy for warm outerwear. For evening wear, it was silk, satin, taffeta, moiré silk or satin, voile, velvet, crêpe de Chine, gold and silver lamé, which was in vogue, either for home dressmaking or for ready-to-wear clothes from the shops.

There were not many man-made fibres but artificial silk was used for underwear and stockings. You could buy artificial silk stockings at Cochrane's in Baxter's Place near the Playhouse for $1/11^{1}/_{2}$d (less than 10 pence). We preferred to pay a little more for Morley's, Aristoc or Bear Brand pure silk stockings, fully fashioned. That is, shaped at the heel, toe and up the calf, for 2/11d (less than 15 pence). You attached them to suspenders on a suspender belt. The seams up the back of the leg had to be dead straight. It was the last thing we made sure of before going out of the front door on a date. Tights had not been invented, except perhaps for ballet dancers! Lisle thread stockings which were quite thick were mostly worn by my mother's generation. We of the younger generation would have died of exposure rather than wear them, even although they were much warmer in the winter than silk.

If a ladder appeared in a stocking, we could have it repaired. In many shops they employed a woman for the job. It must have been a very eye-straining business to climb up the ladder with a fine crochet hook to mend it. It cost very little and there was no shame attached to having mended rips, and darned heels in your stockings or the elbows of your jumpers. The throwaway generation had not been born yet!

Unless in a very informal situation, such as a picnic or sporting event, we all wore hats. Most men did too. Look at any photograph of the time and you will find a sea of hats! Gloves and handbags were also essential for the ladies. They had to "go with" the rest of your outfit, otherwise your best friend would tell you and no mistake. Real leather gloves could be bought for 5/- (25 pence) a pair, and a leather or suede handbag cost about the same. Felt hats were about 3/11d (20p) and to pay as much as 12/11d (65p) was considered outrageous extravagance.

We bought our summer frocks for around 15/- (75p) in the Co-op. or from Maule's at the West End, or Darling's in Princes Street. At Wilkies in Shandwick Place, a suit or a coat cost around 30/- (£1.50). When C&A's opened in Princes Street in the late thirties, a best quality wool coat cost 55/- (£2.75), a summer coat 39/11d (£2). If we had marriage in mind, a bridal dress cost about £6.10/- (£6.50), and a bridesmaid's dress 30/- (£1.50). Shoes and sandals were about 25/- (£1.25) a pair, and all made of leather. We knew of no other material shoes could be made from.

Fur coats were away beyond our pockets. That was something we might aspire to. It was a badge of success. In Patrick Thomson's on the North Bridge, they sold real fur coats for 22 guineas (£23.10p), and you could have a skunk fur cape to wear over your evening gown for 27 guineas (£28.35p).

Our Betty had a silver fox fur. Not a coat, a "tippet". It was the whole animal skin, its four little feet extended, its head with its beady eyes open, and a lovely bushy tail. It was meant to be thrown casually round the shoulders, and a clip under the muzzle fastened the head to the base of the tail. Usually, to be really in fashion, it was allowed to hang off one shoulder. A safety chain prevented it from falling off altogether. It was lined with shiny satin. She paid £3.10/- (£3.50p) for it. Even with the discount she got because she worked in the shop, it was more than a week's wages. She had to borrow from Mother and then pay her back by instalments. My mother had a fur tippet as well, but since, unlike Betty, she cared not a jot about fashion, she wore it like a collar, even in summer. Madeline was the only other member of our family who wore fur, well, not exactly fur — it was a ponyskin jacket. Somehow I never liked it. I could visualise all to clearly its original wearer!

Knitted jumpers and cardigans were about 3/11d (20p) in Blair's Nicolson Street store, and blouses and skirts were a shilling or two more. They appear cheap now, but then our wages were so low that we had to consider very carefully each item we bought, weighing up quality and price. Sometimes, we could pick up bargains at the sales. But our bargain often turned out to be no bargain at ali and we hid our mistakes at the back of the wardrobe!

A hat was the crowning glory of any outfit. Halo hats, which framed the face were all the rage for a year or two. Sailor hats, tricorns, berets, trilbies and bowlers all took their turn. They were decorated with artificial flowers or feathers. The unflattering cloche hats of the twenties were either thrown in the bucket, or worn by frumpy old women over thirty!

All the girls in our family had straight brown hair. Not a natural curl among them. Permanent waving was just coming into vogue but until we could afford that, we made our own arrangements. We wound our hair each night into hard steel curlers before going to bed. We were quite prepared to put up with any discomfort to achieve the style we wanted. From the age of about twelve, I was always experimenting with my hair. Parting it at one side, or the other, keeping it short, or letting it grow, a curly fringe, or a smooth wave over the forehead, an auburn colour rinse instead of my usual "moosey broon". With all the attention I gave my hair, it surprises me that I have so much of it left.

The Amami Company which sold shampoos had an advertising campaign with the slogan "Friday night is Amami night". My generation of women obeyed that as if it was one of the ten commandments!

Although sometimes pushed out of the mainstream of fashion to make room for shorter skirts or other fads, the thirties look never really went away. The forties wartime styles were only a modification of them. The tailored suits in tweed, flannel or linen foreshadowed the Service uniform of wartime.

Makeup had become accepted as normal now. My sisters were always experimenting with it. Mother often called them into the kitchen before they left on a date so that she could see whether they had been too heavy handed with it. Most of the products we used could be bought in Woolworths. First you smeared on a thin layer of Pond's Vanishing Cream, then Côty face powder was applied with a powder puff. We never needed rouge as we all had rosy cheeks without it. The colours of the lipsticks seem a little strong now. There was even black lipstick made by Tangee. Fortunately, it was not black on your lips, but dark red. We seldom used mascara and never eye shadow. That was only used in stage makeup and no respectable girl wore it in the street. We plucked our eyebrows to a thin line, in imitation of the film stars. Too much makeup was a grievous sin and we knew it.

To preserve a smooth skin and never, ever get wrinkles, all we had to do was apply Pond's Cold Cream every night before going to bed. If the young men we fancied had seen us going to bed all greased up and in curlers, they would have run a mile!

We painted our nails occasionally, but it was rather a lot of bother to keep them gleaming and unchipped. My father hated painted nails and often made disapproving remarks about them while we sat round the table at a meal. They put him off his food, he said! He was never pleased either if we were reeking of our latest choice in perfumes such as, "Evening in Paris", or "Californian Poppy". But my father had mellowed a bit by the time I was a teenager, and had long since philosophically accepted that he was outnumbered. He liked a quiet life anyway. Our parents were fairly tolerant of their young family and accepted that things had changed since they were young.

My mother at that time was struggling through most winters against ill health. When we came in from work for tea, we often made our own. We did not mind; it gave us a measure of choice in what we ate. We could bring home chips, or toast bread and cheese under the grill. It was the junk food of the day I suppose. We never went to restaurants or hotels to eat, so we could make no comparisons. We were not "fikey" eaters.

When Mother was well enough to be in charge, she gave us good plain cooking. Thick broth made with stock from a knap bone, or a piece of flank mutton. You could stand your spoon up in it. Her lentil soup was made with a ham shank and was so thick you could cut it into slices when it was cold. We had mince and doughballs with plenty of vegetables and beef stew in lots of gravy with mashed potatoes. My father loved tripe and onions in a thick milky sauce and liver done to a turn, tasty and tender. Kippers were our favourite fish, even although it was difficult to get rid of the smell afterwards. Smoked Finnan haddy steamed in milk went down a treat as well. Sausages, corned beef, bacon and eggs, black pudding, macaroni and cheese, and Heinz baked beans on toast, were all included in our menus. In those days, the tins of baked beans had a little piece of bacon on the top when you opened them and there was usually an argument as to whose turn it was to eat it.

For dessert, we had all the usual milk puddings, semolina, rice with a lovely toasted top, rhubarb or Delmonte tinned peaches with custard. Mother's steamed puddings were really filling. Sometimes she put dried fruit in them, or spooned a dollop of black treacle in the bottom of the pudding basin, so that when it was turned out, the treacle ran invitingly down the sides. On our birthdays, instead of a birthday cake, Mother made us a steamed pudding with one or two silver thrupenny bits wrapped in a scrap of paper in it, bachelor's buttons, wee dolls and other pagan fertility symbols. When one of them landed on our plate we greeted it with great glee, especially if it was a thrupenny bit, a small fortune to us.

Our diet was very simple. We seldom had chicken. Even a large one would not have gone very far among us. For some reason, pork hardly ever appeared either. My mother was not a very imaginative cook and we usually knew what to expect according to the day of the week. As for baking, she used to make lovely girdle scones which we enjoyed eating while they were hot, but apart from that, there were no big baking sessions.

On Saturdays after dinner, we were allowed to have a "shop bought" cake as a treat. Whoever was sent down to Smith's in Lochend Road, or up to the Store Bakery, had to remember the specific kind of cake each one of us fancied. Vanilla cakes, macaroon cakes, snowballs, Empire biscuits, flies' cemeteries, maids of honour were all great favourites with us.

For tea on a Sunday when we were all together, we very often had a salad with Kersans boiled ham. We considered it the best to be had anywhere. In summer Mother used to put it on a plate in a cool corner of our inside stair. On one occasion, our dog sniffed it out and ate the lot! Not a scrap was left for our tea. The dog was in the doghouse.

In winter we often sat around the kitchen fire on dark Sunday afternoons. Sometimes we emptied our purses and pooled what money we had to buy sweets at the corner shop. Then we idled the afternoon away talking, laughing, smoking, eating sweets and listening to the wirelesss.

When we had all grown up and were no longer interested in family picnics, my father sold the car. Probably he was quite glad to give up driving. He had never been an enthusiastic driver and the roads were becoming busier every year. We scarcely noticed its absence, we were so busy pursuing our social lives.

We were allowed to go to the Marine Gardens ballroom in Portobello. There we could mix with the opposite sex. Like our older sisters, we never had dancing lessons. We often danced the evening away with any boy who asked us. Of course, if he was unattractive or, the ultimate horror, you were taller than he, you had to make some excuse to decline his invitation. The boy you danced the last waltz with usually saw you home, even although you had never met him before that evening. Now that may sound a dangerous practice, but we had the confidence of youth that nothing bad could happen to us. Our escort would be lucky if he got a kiss for his trouble, even if he had missed the last tram and had a long way to go home himself. If you hit it off together, another date might be made but if not, we soon recovered from our disappointment.

There were house rules to be observed, of course. We were expected to be home by about 10.30 pm or 11 at the latest. We were expected to let our parents know in advance if we were going to a late dance. One night I recklessly flouted the rules, when a young man who had a car offered to take me to North Berwick, after a dance at the Marines. Now, young men with cars were few and far between, and as it was a beautiful summer evening, I went. When I finally got home, Mother was furious. She forgot I was grown up and gave me a good clout. I forgot too, and accepted it without protest. When I had a steady

149

boyfriend whom she knew and liked, Mother stopped fussing and I did my best to stick to the house rules.

We lived in a very safe environment and apart from accidents, our problems were usually self inflicted. Drink was no problem as we had no cash to spare on it and we knew nothing of drugs. The boys we knew did not have cars. True, we often jumped off trams and buses while they were in motion but everyone did that. Mother and Dad were always around when they were needed. The house stayed the same, the neighbours stayed the same; the shops we used stayed the same; our friends stayed the same; our leisure pursuits stayed the same for many years. In fact, Leith itself stayed the same, in spite of the takeover by Edinburgh. It was only when I left the security of our home to try my wings that I discovered what a hard, cold, unsympathetic, insecure world it sometimes was out there.

We packed all the enjoyment we could into those few years before the war, as if we knew it had to end in tears. We spent a good deal of time in the various picture houses in Edinburgh and Leith. Jim used to go roller-skating at the Marines, but I had seen the bruises Mamie suffered and thought it was too dangerous. Curiously enough, none of us took part in organised sport. My brothers and my father never went to football or rugby matches, and the girls lost interest in tennis after a while. We swam at Portobello Pool in the summer but did not join swimming clubs.

In winter, we still loved the rough and tumble of snowball fights, and sliding recklessly down Lochend Road. But the most enjoyable time of the winter was, of course, Christmas. There were always so many dances and parties to go to. Christmas Day was a general holiday, but not for my father and brothers. It was not until after the Second World War that tradesmen were given a day's holiday for Christmas. Our dinner that day was fairly simple. It did not include turkey or chicken, or Christmas pudding, nor did we have a Christmas tree. These things, and all the trimmings, had not yet been commercially promoted in Scotland. Our mantlepiece was always covered with Christmas cards, and we changed gifts. I always longed for something frivolous, a lovely presentation box of perfume, or a powder compact. But usually we received and gave useful things like, stockings, socks, ties, slippers, or underwear, all items with a useful life before them. We had no sherry before our dinner, nor wine, nor brandy to follow, and it never crossed our minds that we were missing anything.

Hogmanay was a different kettle of fish. We looked forward to that with great anticipation. We actually had sherry, whisky, ginger wine and lemonade in the house. On 31st December when midnight was approaching, Mother always tidied up the house, cleaned out the old ashes from the fire and washed up any dirty dishes. Then she laid out shortbread, black bun, fruit cake and biscuits, and set out the glasses and bottles. Just before the clock struck twelve, my father went out of the front door, and then came in again as the last chime of the old year died away. He chose to ignore the superstition that it was bad luck to first foot your own house! Neighbours sometimes came in to be offered a drink and a New Year handshake. As we grew up, there were boyfriends and girlfriends but never a big party. Soon the younger members left to go "first footing". First we went to the homes of some of our group. You have to take something with you as a gift when you first foot a house, but we were not expected to bring much. Quite often it was a piece of coal or a piece of cake. The darkest member of our chums was pushed into the house first, another superstition.

Often we found ourselves in houses where the host and hostess were strangers to us, and there was always such confusion that introductions were impossible. In each house we were offered a drink of some kind, and sometimes coffee and sandwiches too. We could easily observe what "the drink" could do, as there was usually someone just drunk enough to sing a solo. "The Rose of Trallee" and "Nellie Dean" were very popular in such circumstances!

New Year's Day was a day of recovery for us all, sleeping late, and assembling blearily round the dinner table about 12.30 pm where Mother presided over the traditional beefsteak pie dinner. She had been up for a while by that time, and because everything had been cleaned on Hogmanay, it was a holiday for her too. In the afternoon, other members of our family came to wish us a happy New Year, and in the evening there were calls to be made on people we had missed the night before.

Next day it was back to "parritch an' auld claes", in the knowledge that you had rashly made New Year resolutions you might be unable to keep. Never mind. Another year lay before us. What would it bring? Excitement? Fun? Courtship? Marriage? We were ready for anything.

CHAPTER 16

Count down to war

During the year before war was declared, the people of Leith made their preparations like everyone else in Britain. At a crowded open meeting in Smith's Rooms, the agenda covered how to protect ourselves during an air raid, from possible gas attack, and from possible invasion.

Instructions about the evacuation of children from towns to country districts had been issued on a national scale. We stood patiently in line for gas masks, and then in another line for identity cards. In the newspapers, there were calls for volunteers for ARP wardens, Special Constables, fire-watchers. Most business firms and factories set up their own system of fire watching, ready to be put into effect when war broke out.

Even the fate of household pets was not forgotten and there were instructions as to where you could have your pets humanely destroyed, rather than have them suffer in air raids.

Air raid shelters were being dug in Princes Street Gardens, the Links, and other open spaces. We had our own shelter in our garden. It was made of corrugated iron and issued free by the Government. My father and brothers dug a hole in our small area of grass to fit the shelter. It was dark, gloomy and earth smelling in there. I was only in it once. That was when Leith took a pasting. We sat in the dark quaking at the crack of the anti-aircraft guns, and the thud of the bombs, until the all-clear sounded.

We had no illusions about all these preparations. We knew that war would come, the question was when. There was no feeling of panic and everyone went about their business as usual. If there had to be a war, we intended to be as ready as possible to defend ourselves. This would be different from the First World War when Scotland had seemed so isolated and safe. The world had grown much smaller since then, and we expected to be as vulnerable as England.

We had become accustomed to Hitler's ravings, but we took them seriously now. There had to be a war to stop his jackboots striding all over Europe. Poland was obviously next on his hit list, and after the humiliation of the Munich Pact, we had to be prepared.

The summer of 1939 was one of the happiest of my life. I was going steady. Even the fact that the object of my affections was in the Territorials with our Jim, and would be called up immediately war broke out, failed to spoil my enjoyment of life. Jim, too, was going steady and his girlfriend had become a regular visitor to our house.

It was rather a crazy time, filled with a kind of frenzied activity. The dance halls in Edinburgh and Leith had become infected with two "action" dances called the "Palais Glide" and the "Lambeth Walk". They were not as graceful as the foxtrot or the waltz, but they were great fun. We loved them.

Tennis, bowling or golf clubs often had summer dances. They were called "Flannel Dances". We went in a summer frock and our partners wore flannel trousers, open necked shirts, and a sports jacket. We often had a "Paul Jones" to start off, which gave everyone a chance to change partners. Then there were ladies' choices and "excuse me" dances so that there was every opportunity to meet as many members of the opposite sex as possible.

Portobello open air pool was crammed with happy bathers and there were galas in the evening. Sometimes there was midnight bathing too. It had an atmosphere all its own, and there were always queues on its first day of opening for the summer months.

Our Jim had a tandem around that time. One day he persuaded me to go on the back of it, while he controlled the front end. We zoomed through Restalrig Village at breakneck speed. I was too terrified even to scream. When we began to slow down at the crossroads, a policeman stepped out into the road and stopped us. He gave us a right telling off but allowed us to continue on our way, on foot. He was a reckless idiot at times, my brother Jim. Once when we were on holiday, he shot me in the leg with an air gun by mistake, at least I hope it was a mistake. No great damage was done but I had the mark of it for years. One Christmas day he broke Jean's brand new doll. He still remembers the tears and lamentations which followed. He was definitely accident prone in his youth.

During the pre-war summer, we often went to the cheapest seats in the "gods" at the various theatres. The Wilson Barrett Company was at the Empire with "Love from a Stranger". Dave Willis was pulling them in at the King's in the "Halfpast eight show". Victoria Hopper was appearing at the Lyceum in "The Boy David", and Jack Radcliffe's Summer Show was knocking them in the aisles at the Royal. It was the time of the big dance band shows. We had heard them on the radio, so we wanted to see them in the flesh. We were not disappointed.

A night at the pictures was still a favourite pastime. We queued for more than an hour to see Walt Disney's "Snow White and the Seven Dwarfs" at the Regal. Fred Astaire and Ginger Rogers' dancing and singing in "Roberta", and Judy Garland and Mickey Rooney in "Babes in Arms" took our minds off the international situation. Deanna Durbin's lovely voice enchanted us in "Three Smart Girls". We shed tears of laughter at the Marx Brothers in "Room Service", and tears of emotion with Bette Davis in "Dark Victory".

In our house, all these shows and films were discussed in detail when my married sisters came to call. The songs were studied to get the words right so that we could sing them. "Let's call the whole thing off", "Lovely to look at", "Change partners", "Smoke gets in your eyes", "A fine romance", "Nice work if you can get it", all those and many more evoke that period very vividly. Their lyrics even passed my father's severe tests! We bought the sheet music sometimes at 3d or 6d each. If you went to Methven Simpson's in Princes Street, they employed a pianist to help you choose your music by playing it for you.

We could not have guessed how nostalgic these songs were to become in later years for our generation. For many, they would bring back a poignant or painful memory of someone far away, or killed in the war.

Our interest in Hollywood personalities was not limited to the stars. We knew many of the supporting or character actors like Mischa Auer, tall and excitable. Then there was Walter Connolly, fat and paunchy, usually a father figure. Elisha Cook and Peter Lorre we always immediately identified as "baddies" from their sinister looks. Basil Rathbone was a rather elegant villain, and S. Z. Szakal was a lovable, cuddly, middle European. We recognised them as they appeared regularly in lots of films, although sometimes we could not put a name to them.

At the Playhouse that summer, they were showing Jeanette MacDonald in "Serenade"; and at the Ritz The Ritz Brothers in "The Three Musketeers". At our local, the Capital, it was Jack Oakie in "Thanks for everything"; the second feature was Peter Lorre in "Mr Motto's last warning". The New Victoria, always referred to by us as the 'New Vic' was offering a midnight matinee starting at 11.15 pm with "The Mikado". These happy films full of wisecracking dialogue, beautiful people in smart clothes, and wonderful music, sent us home content, in spite of the gloomy newsreels.

We loved dancing too, and Carroll Gibbons and his Savoy Orpheans were appearing at the Marine Gardens. There was speedway racing and roller skating there too. We all had our favourite dance halls. Of course, if you were going steady, you had no need of the dance halls to introduce you to members of the opposite sex. Instead, you went with your partner to the pictures to sit near the back and hold hands. It was not the done thing to hold hands or kiss in public.

Jim went off with his regiment to Towyn in Wales for their fortnight's "Terry" camp. By this time, we knew that Hitler and Stalin had signed a "non-aggression pact" and were preparing to carve up the rest of Europe between them, starting with Poland. The British Ambassador delivered to Hitler, Britain's response that "whatever may prove to be the nature of the Moscow agreement, it cannot alter Great Britain's obligation to Poland". So our boats were burned. Hitler confidently waited for Britain to step aside and leave Poland to him. But Britain and France stood firm. Hitler must have been surprised. He never learned from this lesson and often in the war years completely misunderstood and misinterpreted the feelings of the British people.

Towards the end of August, there was a rehearsal of the evacuation procedures, and an appeal for more helpers was issued. It was received by the citizens of Edinburgh and Leith with complete apathy. Perhaps the expectation of sudden death from the air might have had something to do with that attitude. Probably people wanted to be at home when the first bombs fell, rather than looking after strangers' children. There is no doubt that we expected to be bombed in the first days, or even the first hours, of the war.

My mother and father were in their fifties now and had been married for over thirty years. They said very little to us of their feelings at the approach of another war in their lives. Perhaps they were a bit more silent and grim lipped than usual. Memories of the First World War must have been very vivid to them. Jimmy's death; the terror of the air raids; the privation of inadequate food and heat. They knew what war was like, and dreaded another.

To my married sisters and brother, a war would bring unwelcome changes. Instead of settling down to rear children with their husbands, my sisters might be left to cope alone. How long would their husbands be gone? Would they be in the fighting line? Would they be in aeroplanes, or on the high seas? What future did they have? How could they manage on a serviceman's wife's allowance. If they had those thoughts, they put up with them in silence. In our family we were not expected to moan about our lot, just to get on with it.

We three unmarried young people were completely indifferent to the worries of Mother and Dad, or our sisters and older brother. We were immortal. Here was a challenge and we accepted it. What if bombs fell? What if one of us were to be killed on active service? We thought we were invincible.

In the last few tension-filled days, some members of our family were immediately affected by the proximity of war. The evacuation of children from Edinburgh, the real thing this time and not a rehearsal, began at 7 am on 1st September. Thirty thousand children assembled at their various rendez-vous, carrying the minimum of personal possessions, to be documented and issued with identification labels and a packed lunch. Many of the mothers had elected to accompany their child into voluntary exile and my sister Netta was one of these. She and her two year old daughter joined other mothers and children at Abbeyhill Station. They had no idea where they were going. They boarded a train which took them to West Linton. There they were taken to a hall to be allocated places in the surrounding countryside. Netta and her daughter were driven in a private car to a farm cottage at Callands. Annie, who welcomed them to her cottage, had been a cook up at the "big hoose" and was now retired, She became a good friend to them and made their stay a happy one until they came back to Edinburgh a year later. It must have been a harrowing experience for many of these children to be separated from everything they knew. It's not surprising that many of them returned to Edinburgh within a week or two to face whatever came, rather than be cut off from their homes.

Betty's husband had joined the Royal Navy in April of that year and they were living in Southampton in rented accommodation. One day during the week before war was declared, he went off in the morning saying to Betty as he left, "I'll come home early tonight and we'll go and see 'The Four Feathers'" (that was a popular film at the time with John Clements in it). Her husband failed to come home that night. She had no news whatsoever of him for about three weeks. Then she had word from him that he was with *HMS Maidstone,* but of course, for security reasons, he could not tell her where he was. She could only write to him "care of GPO London".

His ship did not return to Britain until the following Spring and only then could he tell her he had been half way across the world and back. Soon he was off again and as she had no idea when she would see him again, she eventually packed everything up and returned to Leith for the birth of her first child.

My brother Jim's regiment terminated their training in Wales and returned to Edinburgh. Not to the bosom of his family, however. His regiment was stationed in and around Portobello to await further orders. It was a strange time for them. They were often on guard duties and without sleep for long periods. They had an anti-aircraft gun on the roof of the Ramsay Tech. and had to "stand to" whenever an alert was on. In a way, they were luckier than the civilian population, as all they had to do was to obey orders from their superior officers. Nothing else was expected of them.

Hitler invaded Poland and Britain sent an ultimatum stating that if German troops were not removed from Poland, war would be declared. Hitler thought he could ignore the ultimatum and get away with it. He was wrong. Our children were gone. Our men were in the process of going. There was a complete blackout as from 2nd September. Edinburgh and Leith were disfigured by sandbags and shelters. We had to remember to carry our gas masks everywhere. We faced the prospect of sudden death and destruction from the air at worst, and inconvenience, separation from our loved ones, and discomfort at best. But we knew where we stood now and there was no looking back. It was no surprise to us when at 11 am on Sunday the 3rd, Neville Chamberlain announced on the wireless that we were at war.

I was in Portobello that morning. It was a lovely day, sunny and warm for the time of year. Blue sky above and no wind. Suddenly we heard the wail of the air raid sirens. We had heard them often enough before in practices, but now we were at war. Was this to be our first taste of aerial warfare? In the streets, people hurried along, anxious to get home. The trams were filled to overflowing. There was no panic, but the feeling was that if we were going to be bombed and killed, we would rather be at home with our families. What a relief it was when we heard the "all clear" sound.

During the following week, the schools were closed, so were the cinemas and theatres. No sporting events took place. Food and fuel controls were introduced. Gradually we adapted to our new situation. The cinemas and theatres eventually opened again to make an important contribution to our morale.

Suddenly, at a stroke, our house was practically empty of children. Only Jean and I were left and very soon we joined the services. Eventually Mother and Dad were alone together and back where they had started so many years before. But not for long. Our house became a refuge for those members of the family made temporarily homeless.

Charlie and his wife sought shelter with Mother and Dad for a while when they were bombed out of their house. Leith was attacked from the air and a landmine fell on David Kilpatrick's school next to them. Then Betty stayed at Woodbine, until she found a place of her own while her husband was at sea. Madeline came to stay from Aberdeen when her husband was called up. And, of course, Jean and I came home when we had a ten day leave every three months.

In spite of war time conditions, nothing could stop the happy events occurring in our family. When the war started my parents had three grandchildren. By the end of the war, they had ten. So our numbers began to increase once more, a trend which still continues to this day.

When the war in Europe ended in May 1945, the members of our family slowly began to return to Edinburgh and Leith. I was the first to be released in July from the ATS. My sisters' husbands returned from far away places to be demobilised in their turn. Some of them came back to children they had had very little contact with during the war years. Our Jim had married before he went out to the Middle East with his regiment. He was there for more than four years. He returned to Scotland in August 1945 to meet the daughter he had never seen, and was not released until April 1946.

Mother and Dad were thankful to see us all return whole and healthy. The war had taken its toll of them. My father was teaching woodwork in a school now. The work he had been doing for the meat packing business had dried up completely with war time rationing, and since there was a serious shortage of teachers, he had stepped in to that occupation. My mother's health was more precarious than ever. Food rationing had not helped her, although my father did without some of his own rations to give to her. There was a black market, of course, but my parents knew nothing of that and, I suspect, would not have taken advantage of it if they had.

For a while our house was busy again. There was always some married member of the family staying temporarily until they found a home of their own. We were all married now and eager to get on with our lives which had been interrupted by six years of war. Eventually, Mother and Dad's long years of parenthood were at an end, and the two of them were on their own again.

Now, when their children look back on their lives in a more objective light, we all realise how lucky we were to have had such a secure and happy childhood and young adulthood. We were never "feather-bedded", but never deprived of the important things in life such as love and support. These were given to us without lavish and sentimental displays of affection. That was not my parents' way. But we have never had any doubt that our parents loved each other and each one of us, in spite of the many times we must have annoyed or disappointed them. No children could ask for a better beginning.

Appendix

These rhymes, games and songs are reproduced by kind permission of James T.R. Ritchie from "The Singing Street" and "Golden City", published by Oliver & Boyd, Edinburgh.

Action Rhymes

The beists in your heid

See a' the beists in your heid,
See the wee drap in mine:
See a' the beists in your heid,
See — there's nane in mine!

Start off with some sand on the palm of your hand, throw it into the air and catch less of it on back of hand, repeat until no sand left.

Incy wincy spider

Incy wincy spider
Climbing up the spout:
Down came the rain
And washed the spider out.

Out came the sun
And dried up all the rain:
Incy wincy spider
Climbed the spout again.

The forefinger of one hand is placed on the thumb of the other, and the thumb of this hand on the forefinger of the other. With the topmost touching fingers as centre, the lower fingers keep swivelling round so that the spider climbing up and down is simulated.

One two three four five

One two three four five
Once I caught a fish alive.
Why did you let him go?
Because he bit my finger so.

With a small child — grip each of its fingers in turn finishing with the pinkie which you squeeze a wee bit harder.

Two little Dicky-Birds

Two little dicky-birds
Sitting on a wall:
One named Peter:
One named Paul:

Fly away Peter
Fly away Paul:
Come back Peter
Come back Paul.

"Peter" & "Paul" (each a small piece of paper) are stuck to the nails of the two forefingers, and the "birds" fly away because the bare second fingers take their places. Reversing this "Peter" and "Paul" return.

Round & Round the Garden

Round and round the garden
I lost my Teddy Bear:
One step, two step,
And tickle you under there!

First two lines are played with the forefinger on the child's palm, the third line on the forearm, the last under the arm.

Ball games

Ala Bala Ala Bala

Ala bala Ala bala,
Who's got the ball?
I haven't got it
In my pocket:
Ala bala Ala bala,
Who's got the ball?

One player stands out with ball hidden in hands; the rest stand in a row hands cupped; passing along the row reciting the rhyme, she surreptitiously drops the ball into someone's hands. The player on whom the rhyme ends guesses who's got the ball. If right it's her turn to stay out; if not the original player carries on.

One two three a-leerie

One two three a-leerie
Four five six a-leerie
Seven eight nine a-leerie:
Ten a-leerie, postman!

Right leg over ball.
Left over ball.
Right leg again.
Left leg again & at postman, birl before you catch the ball.

Open the gates & let me in, sir
Open the gates & let me in, sir
Open the gates & let me in, sir
early in the morning!

or

I am your master.

With each "Open", lift your leg over ball, right & left legs turn about.
Birl as in first verse.

Plainie Clappie

Plainie	Stot the ball against wall
Clappie	Clap hands
Rollie-pin	Roll hands over each other
To backie	Hands clapped behind back
Right hand	Ball caught in right hand
Left hand	Ball caught in left hand
High si-toosh	Ball caught with clasped hands upturned
Low-si-toosh	Ball caught with clasped hands down turned
Telephone	Hand held to ear
The answer	Hand held to mouth
Touch my heel	Hand must touch heel
Touch my toe	Hand must touch toe
Through ye go	Ball goes through legs
Big birly-o	Turn round once before catching ball

Catchphrases

"Does your Mother know you're out?"

"All dressed up and nowhere to go!"

"And the band played 'Believe it if you like!'"

"It's your eyes, ducky, it's your eyes!"

"One foot in the grave, and the other on a banana skin!"

"Edge your barrie".

"Let's all go down the Strand — have a banana!"

"What's that got to do with the cars going up the Mound!"

"Umpa umpa, stick it up your jumper!"

"Tarzan! was all the apes could say!"

Counting out Rhymes

One two three four

One two three four
Mary at the cottage door:
Five six seven eight
Eating cherries off a plate.

Eetle Ottle

Eetle ottle black bottle
eetle ottle out:
If you want a piece in jam
Please step out.

My Wee Jeanie

My wee Jeanie
had a nice clean peenie
And guess what colour it was?
Red
R-E-D spells red and if you have it on
you go out of this game.

One potato two potato

One potato,two potato,three potato,four:
Five potato,six potato,seven potato,more!

Players hold out clenched fists, and the one who counts out the rhyme also has her fists clenched. As she strikes each fist in turn with her fist, she keeps chanting the couplet. On whatever fist the word "more" falls, that fist gets tucked behind the player's back. If the Counter-out happens to get two of her fists tucked behind her back, she counts with nods of her head. Whoever is left with one or two potatoes held out is "het".

Eenie Meenie

Eenie Meenie Mynnie mo
Sit the baby on the po
When he's done, wipe his bum
Eenie Meenie Mynnie mo.

Games

Knock Knock

Knock Knock!
Who's there?
Rose.
Rose who?
Rows o' housis! etc.

What's the time Mr Wolf?

One person is the Wolf, and the whole line of players are behind him and they shout "What's the time Mr Wolf?" and if he says "3 o'clock" nothing happens, but if he says "12 o'clock" that's his dinner time and everybody runs away because if he catches you he puts you into the dinner pot. 5 o'clock can be the Wolf's tea time and 9 o'clock his supper time.

A-Leevoy

One player is het and has a den, and he has to catch all the others and put them in his den; but all the prisoners may be set free by any player still at large by creeping and thrusting a foot across the line of the den. At that moment he cries out "A-leevoy!"

Pass the parcel

Used mostly at parties. Stand in a circle and pass a parcel to music. When the music stops, whoever is holding the parcel is out. When one person is left he/she gets the contents of the parcel.

Kick the can

You start off by throwing the can away and the person who's het retrieves it and replaces it in the den, hiding his eyes and counting up to an agreed number. The other players hide. When anyone is spied there's a race to the can, which the spier must touch before the others can kick it.

Songs and Rhymes

Hallow'een

Tramp, tramp, tramp the boys are marching,
We are the guisers at the door;
If you dinnie let us in
We'll bash your windies in
And ye'll never the see the guisers any more!

Prayer

This night when I lie down to sleep,
I pray thee, Lord, my soul to keep;
If I should die before I wake,
I pray thee, Lord my soul to take.

Skipping rhymes

Grannie in the kitchen

Grannie in the kitchen
Doin' some stitchin'
In comes a bogey man
And chases grannie oot!

I'm a Girl Guide

I'm a Girl Guide
Dressed in blue
See all the actions
I can do.

Salute to the east
And bow to the west
And turn my back on the sailor boys.

Jelly on the Plate

Jelly on the plate
Jelly on the plate;
Wiggle-waggle, wiggle-waggle
Jelly on the plate.

JAM YESTERDAY

Charlie Chaplin

The moon shines bright on Charlie Chaplin
His boots are crackin'
For the want o' black'nin'
And his baggy troosers needin' mendin'
Before they send him
To the Dardanelles!

The big ship

The big ship sails through the Eely-Alley-O
The Eely-Alley-O, the Eely-Alley-O;
The big ship sails through the Eely-Alley-O
on the fourteenth of December..

Old soldiers

Old soldiers never die,
Never die, never die;
Old soldiers never die
They only fade away.

Amy Johnson

Amy Johnson flew in an airyplane
She flew to China and never came back again;
She flew in an old Tin Lizzie
Enough to make her dizzy;
She looks so sweet upon the seat
Of an airyplane built for two.

There were fleas

There were fleas, fleas
Wi' kilts and hairy knees
in the stores, in the stores.
There were fleas, fleas
Wi' kilts and hairy knees
In the Quartermaster's stores.

Chorus

My eyes are dim I cannot see
I have not got my specs with me
I have not got my specs with me!

There were rats, rats
in bowler hats and spats, etc.

No more clay pipes

No more clay pipes
Nothing but cigars,
Now that I'm a driver
on the tramway cars!

Chap at the door

Chap at the door
Keek in
Lift the sneck
And walk in.

JAM YESTERDAY

There was a wee man

There was a wee man
Who lived in a pan
The pan was too wee
So he lived in the sea
The sea was too wide
So he lived in the tide
And 'a the wee fishes
Ran up his backside!

Singing Games

Here's a poor widow

Here's a poor widow she's left alone
She has no money to marry upon
Come choose to the east
Come choose to the west
Come choose to the one that you love best.

Now they're married we wish them joy
Every year a girl and a boy
Loving each other
Like sister and brother
To play the game at kissing-the-gether.

For the first verse the the girls dance round the "widow" in the centre who picks her "sweetheart". The second verse then starts up, the two in the centre kiss, and then the game begins again with the sweetheart as the new widow.

Adree Adree I dropped it

I sent a letter to my love
And on the way I dropped it;
Someone must have picked it up
And put it in their pocket
Adree adree adree
Adree adree adree
I dropped it.

All sit in a circle and the one that's out goes round the outside of the circle with a hopping step, a hanky in her hand. She drops it behind someone as the verse ends. Whoever discovers it has to chase the dropper. If she's caught she's out again. If she gets to the empty place in the circle, the other is het.